Parenting
THE BEST THAT YOU CAN BE

Nancy Van Pelt

First published in 2017.
Copyright © 2017 The Stanborough Press Ltd.

All rights reserved.
No part of this publication may be reproduced
in any form without prior permission from the publisher.

British Library Cataloguing in Publication Data.
A catalogue record for this book is
available from the British Library.

ISBN 978-1-78665-017-7
Published by
The Stanborough Press Ltd.,
Grantham, Lincolnshire, England.
Designed by Slaviša Tešović.
Printed in Serbia.

Unless otherwise stated, Bible quotations are taken from
The New International Version (Hodder and Stoughton).
Other versions used, indicated by initials:
NRSV = New Revised Standard Version (Oxford)
NLT = New Living Translation (Tyndale)
TLB = The Living Bible (Kingsway)
KJV = King James Version

Important note: Unless otherwise obvious from the
immediate context, all personal pronouns such as he, she,
him or her should not be regarded as excluding the other
gender.

What's inside?

Before you begin — 7

Chapter 1: — 15
Help your child develop positive self-worth

Chapter 2: — 39
Communication is the key

Chapter 3: — 47
Obedience: Developing your strategies

Chapter 4: — 63
What counts is character

Chapter 5: — 89
How to face divorce, single parenting and blended families

Chapter 6: — 101
A good plan for smart families

SMART PARENT

Before you begin

> 'Having children makes you no more a parent than having a piano makes you a pianist.' Michael Levine

> 'Parenthood is a long-term investment, not a short-term loan.'
> Anonymous

> 'Keep these words that I am commanding you today in your heart. Recite them to your children and talk about them when you are at home and when you are away, when you lie down and when you rise.'
> Deuteronomy 6:6, 7, NRSV

Hit television shows like **Nanny 911** and **Super Nanny** give us a peek behind the scenes at parents who haven't a clue about how to handle their children. While being both entertaining and discouraging, such shows feature nearly hopeless mums and dads being coached by smart nannies.

'No, it isn't OK for your child to throw things at you when he gets upset.'

'Yes, it is OK for you to set a time for the children to turn off the TV and get to bed.'

'It might be good for you and your husband to consider not throwing things at each other, especially when the children are around.'

How clueless can some parents be? Yet occasionally we still get a glimpse of a few successful, happy parents who seem especially good at handling their children. Ever wonder how they do it?

I am the parent of three adult children who are now raising children of their own. I am a mother, grandmother and certified family life educator who has written some forty-two books on family issues and taught hundreds of parenting seminars over a span of twenty-five years. I write today as one concerned parent to another.

Through parenting my own children, personal study, teaching hundreds of parent workshops and counselling hundreds of parents I have identified some common core principles that S-M-A-R-T parents can follow.

If you want to become a **smart** parent, and feel happier and more in control of yourself as you parent, try this experiment:

PARENTING: THE BEST THAT YOU CAN BE

for the next few weeks, pretend that you live according to the following principles . . .

S **Stay open to new methods of parenting.** In the book **Who Moved My Cheese?** Spenser Johnson points out a difference between people and mice. When mice discover that something they are doing doesn't work, they try something else. But when humans find that what they are doing isn't working, they get irritated and angry, and give up. Suggest a new approach to such parents and they get defensive or give excuses, and tell you why that approach won't work: 'No, that won't work because . . .'

Instead of resisting change, **smart** parents recognise that a whole new range of possibilities and strategies are open to them. Use whatever you've got at your disposal to make something work. A new way of doing things could make a big difference in your parenting skills. A certain mathematical equation may equal 8; however, there are several ways of arriving at the answer: 4 + 4, 5 + 3, 6 + 2, 7 + 1 and 8 + 0. All equal 8. Stay open to new ways of solving old dilemmas.

M **Make mistakes.** Yes, I give you permission to make mistakes: it's not mistakes that will hurt your child. It's when you stop learning from them. Until then, every mistake you make gives you valuable information regarding success or failure with your child. Every mistake is a learning opportunity in disguise. So when you try a new approach with your child and it doesn't work, **smart** parents will simply try a new approach until they find one that works.

So think of the mistakes you make along the way as stepping stones to success. This will take the negative charge out of setbacks. Mistakes are little more than essential road signs in your journey to becoming a **smart** parent.

A **Act.** Failing to act on what you learn would be like getting wise advice from a leading authority on a vitally important topic and failing to do anything about it. Let's say that my family is worried over my weight gain and personal health. So they give me a copy of **The New Encyclopedia of Weight Loss** by the queen of weight-loss failures, Oprah Winfrey. A couple of months later they ask how I'm doing. 'Terrific,' I tell them with a beaming smile, 'it's a great book. I've read it from cover to cover. I get up early every morning and read a few pages before breakfast. I've memorised a few paragraphs and even meet with a group of weight-loss buddies on Wednesday night. We talk about strategies for losing weight over waffles with berries and whipped cream, doughnuts, milkshakes and pie and ice-cream.'

'But,' they ask, 'are you losing any weight?'
'Huh?'

'Are you doing what the book says to lose weight?' they press. 'Are you cutting back on calories and walking every day?'

'Hardly,' I reply, 'I'm a busy person and that would take too much time. I'd have to change my eating habits, and that would be extremely difficult and almost painful to do. I'm all for weight-loss though. Way too many people are overweight. I believe the book holds valuable information that other people should act on. I just don't have the time.'

I'm reminded of the words from James: **'. . . don't just listen to God's word. You must do what it says. Otherwise, you are only fooling yourselves.'** (James 1:22, NLT.) In other words, take action!

R **Repeat a smarter habit for twenty-one days.** Dr Maxwell Maltz, author of **Psycho-Cybernetics,** states that – regardless of a person's age or sex – it takes twenty-one to forty-five days to change a habit. Through his work as a plastic surgeon,

Maltz discovered that in virtually every case involving amputation it took his patient twenty-one days to lose the ghost image of the missing limb. He studied the correlation between the human mind and the twenty-one-day period and proved scientifically that an idea or action must be repeated for twenty-one consecutive days before it becomes permanently fixed in the subconscious.

You can prove Maltz's theory true or false in the next twenty-one days by working to establish new habits in interacting with your child. For example, if you need to become more positive rather than negative with your child, set aside the next twenty-one days as a test time. Reward yourself in some small way every day for holding your tongue and not screaming. Once you stop making excuses for yourself and become aware of your habits, you can focus on the positive attributes you have as a parent. In three weeks you could be a smarter parent! That twenty-one days is going to pass anyway. Why not give it a shot?

T **Take time to pray daily.** Taking time daily for prayer is absolutely essential in managing a Christian home. Prayer will provide an advantage as you begin to implement the new strategies found in **Parenting**. Regularly submitting your plans to God will help you stick with your objectives in raising a child for as long as it takes to achieve them.

Prayer helps control self-defeating habits, attitudes and impulsive behaviours. Prayer increases faith in your ability to achieve your goal of becoming the firm and loving parent you want to be. Prayer gives strength to endure the daily frustrations of dealing with the immature behaviour of a child, the stress and even the occasional failures on your part.

And remember, before Thomas Edison succeeded in inventing the light bulb, he failed thousands of times. Rather than giving up when he failed, he visualised himself being closer to a working solution. Abraham Lincoln, the president who guided the United States through the most devastating experience in its national history – the Civil War – was defeated many times when he ran for office. Robert Kennedy, a brother of J. F. K. who became a successful US senator in his own right, failed the third grade and was unable to handle a newspaper delivery route successfully. Babe Ruth, the legendary baseball player who played twenty-two seasons and hit 714 home runs, also had a high strike-out rate, yet he is remembered for his successes, not his strikeouts. Edward Gibson, an astronaut chosen for the Skylab IV mission, failed the first and fourth grades.

Failures, disappointments and setbacks are a part of life. **Smart** parents understand that.

PARENTING: THE BEST THAT YOU CAN BE

They recognise that, even when they take two steps forwards and one back, they are still moving towards their goal. Keep your eyes on your successes, whether large or small, rather than being swallowed up by your failures.

From your mistakes, learn what works with your child and what doesn't. But celebrate your successes. Press towards your goal of raising a responsible, well-behaved child with strong values – a child that you and others will enjoy having around. Remain confident in your ability to be more successful in only three weeks. Much of what you accomplish in the next twenty-one to forty-five days depends on your attitude and whether you believe you can do it.

You could be like the person who is afraid of water and, when seeing a large wave coming in his direction, panics and runs, only to be caught, knocked down and crushed by the cold, rushing water: or you can be like the surfer who anticipates the giant wave, prepares to meet it, rises above it and rides it successfully! Your children are the stars in your crown. It is time for these stars to begin to shine. When they shine, so will you. My challenge to you today is to step up to the plate and accept the daunting task of parenting the way God intended.

Your family is your major priority right now. Commit yourself to it. It won't always be easy. It won't always be fun. But it will be worth it in the end when you achieve the success you seek.

Nancy van Pelt

The Good Parent Test

FROM TRAIN UP A CHILD

Are you a good parent? Are you really successful in dealing with the problems that arise daily? Here's a fun test that will measure your current knowledge and ability. Don't take the test too seriously. Just enjoy it!

There are few all-right or all-wrong answers, but if you study the responses carefully you will find one more nearly correct than the others.

If you have children at home, answer each question according to how you would respond now, not how you think you should respond. If you plan to be a parent some day, answer the questions as you think you would function. If your children are grown, answer as you acted back then.

If you were in a doctor's surgery and had to wait before seeing the doctor, what would you be likely to do while waiting?

1. Supervise my child's play
2. Chat to someone in the waiting room
3. Read a popular glamour magazine from the table
4. Read a parenting magazine from the table

The most valuable gift I as a parent can give to my child is:

1. Self-respect
2. Love
3. Discipline
4. Quality time

I frequently discuss and seek child-rearing advice from:

1. No one
2. Friends and relatives
3. Books and seminars
4. 2 and 3

If my child frequently cried because the other children at school didn't like him, I would:

1. Help him find a special talent or compensating skill
2. Talk with his teacher about it
3. Spend more time with him
4. Talk with his friends about it

Positive feelings of worth in your child can best be built by:

1. Utilising natural consequences
2. Talking and listening more
3. Spending quality time with your child
4. Helping your child feel special, loved, and a secure part of your family

On average, how much time a week do you spend communicating with your child one-to-one without TV or other interruptions?

1. More than one hour
2. 31 to 60 minutes
3. 11 to 30 minutes
4. 10 minutes or less

If my child moped around the house complaining there was no one to play with and nothing to do, I would probably:

1. Send him to his room to play
2. Give him a job to do
3. Stop my work and play with him
4. Listen to the feeling behind his complaints

PARENTING: THE BEST THAT YOU CAN BE

If I were watching my favourite programme on TV and my child, without asking permission, switched channels, I would probably say:

1. 'I feel very irritated when my favourite TV programme is interrupted because this is the only relaxation I get all day.'
2. 'Hey, let's be considerate of one another. Please change it back to my programme.'
3. 'Change it back to my programme or you'll get a smack.'
4. 'Can't you see that I am watching a special programme, you idiot?'

If I called my child for dinner and she continued to play rather than coming, I would:

1. Go to her and forcibly bring her to the table
2. Threaten her
3. Call her again
4. Allow her to miss the meal and go ahead without her

If my child were to throw a temper tantrum, I would probably:

1. Ignore her
2. Imitate her by throwing one too
3. Deprive her of a favourite activity or toy
4. Smack her

Parents tend to blame themselves for their child's behaviour, and rightly so, because it is mostly dependent upon:

1. Heredity
2. Using proper child-training methods
3. Parental example and environment
4. Individual temperament type and how parents relate to it

In order to instil pure character traits a parent must develop in a child:

1. Moral excellence
2. A pleasing personality
3. Talent and/or genius
4. A pleasant disposition and individuality

Responsible behaviour and better habits can best be accomplished through:

1. Natural consequences
2. Consistent rules
3. Parental example and a loving home
4. Rewarding positive behaviour and ignoring negative behaviour

The best way of controlling a 17-year-old's choice of questionable peers is to:

1. Invite the questionable friends to your home
2. Move the family away from the area
3. Restrict their privileges
4. Forbid the association

If my 15-year-old failed to clean his room and accept responsibility for common household tasks, I would:

1. Clean the room and do chores for him
2. Allow natural consequences to take over
3. Send an 'I-statement' about my feelings
4. Try to motivate him through a contract system that manipulates privileges

The most effective means of keeping a youngster from experimenting with drugs is:

1. To provide the security of a loving, well-adjusted family life
2. To send him to Christian schools
3. To select his peer group carefully

Before you begin

4. To know the physical symptoms connected with drug abuse

It is now common knowledge that there is a direct link between delinquency and poor nutrition. Which of the following can be attributed to faulty nutrition?

1. Reading problems
2. Hyperactivity
3. Running away and vandalising property
4. All of the above

The best way of handling sibling rivalry is:

1. Let children settle their own disputes
2. Love each child equally
3. Listen to both sides before punishing
4. Protect young children from older ones

The diet our Creator chose for us consists of:

1. Meats and poultry
2. Grains and nuts
3. Fruits and vegetables
4. 2 and 3

Your 7-year-old asks you where babies come from. You would probably respond:

1. 'Babies are made when the daddy puts his penis into the vagina of the mummy. During certain days of the month the mummy can become pregnant and a baby begins to grow in her uterus.'
2. 'When parents want a baby, they love each other in a special way and they'll have one.'
3. 'I'll tell you about it when you get a little older. Remember to ask again.'
4. 'Babies are delivered by the stork.'

Your 5-year-old asks what it is the two of you do after you close the door of your bedroom at night. You would probably respond:

1. 'I never asked my parents questions like that when I was a child.'
2. 'Ask your mother (or father)!'
3. 'We sleep mostly. Why do you ask?'
4. 'Sometimes we sleep and sometimes we love each other in a special way and we want a private place to do it.'

Bringing children into the family:

1. Produces added stress for couples throughout child-rearing years for those not prepared for the task
2. Decreases material satisfaction, particularly during the children's teen years
3. Is more satisfying to women than men
4. Automatically increases marriage satisfaction

Turn to page 14 to score the Good Parent Test.

13

PARENTING: THE BEST THAT YOU CAN BE

Answer Key

THE GOOD PARENT TEST

Scoring:
For all yellow statements, total the point value of the numbers circled.
Enter score here ....

Reverse score on red statements as follows: if the number circled reads (4) receives 1 point; (3) receives 2 points; (2) receives 3 points; (1) receives 4 points.

Total and enter score here ....
Total of both yellow and red ....

Interpretation of Scores:

82 to 88
You are a good parent! But you still will find help in this book.

75 to 81
You are honourable in your child-rearing knowledge. The book will encourage you.

68 to 74
You are acceptable in your child-rearing knowledge, but there is room for improvement.

61 to 67
Your child-rearing knowledge definitely needs help.

52 to 60
You have reprehensible knowledge of parent skills and desperately need help!

A score below 52 is abominable and means that you are violating the majority of principles needed in successful parenting. But take heart. Help is on the way. And there's no better time to begin than now!

After reading the book, please retake the Good Parent Test and re-score yourself to measure your improvement. See, we told you help was on the way!

CHAPTER 1

Help your child develop positive self-worth

> '. . . but bring them up in the discipline and instruction of the Lord.'
> Ephesians 6:4, NRSV

> 'Self-esteem isn't a lesson you teach; it's a quality you nurture.'
> Dr Ronald Levant and John Kelly

In the **Peanuts** comic series, Lucy often assumes the role of a psychiatrist. The cost for her advice is only a nickel. Charlie Brown approaches:

'What can I do for you, Charlie Brown?' she enquires.

'I'm confused,' he replies, 'I can't seem to find a direction, a purpose for life.'

Lucy dispenses her cheap wisdom. 'Oh, don't worry, Charlie Brown. It's like being on a big ocean liner making its way through the sea. Some folks position their deckchairs to face the bow of the ship, and others place their chairs to face the side of the ship or the back of the ship. Which way do you face, Charlie Brown?'

'I can't even unfold the deckchair,' Charlie sadly responds.

Not only can Charlie Brown not unfold the deckchair, he can't make a good throw. Bad things always happen to him; he never gets a Valentine card or gift and can't fly a kite. After falling down, he picks himself up and falls down all over again. Lucy's always putting him down. The little red-haired girl totally ignores him. He makes mistakes and carries the humiliation forever. After all this, he concludes that nobody likes him and comments, 'I guess I'll always be second-rate.'

> **Through the Peanuts series, the late Charles Schultz provides an insightful cartoon for examining self-worth through the eyes of Charlie Brown – a boy who experienced the crushing blows of inferiority on a daily basis. The series, based on Schultz's recollection of humiliation he experienced in life, helps us recall unbearable blunders that we also suffered.**

We laugh because it is all so true. Charlie Brown's unusual perception allows him to worry about his inferiority out loud to his

PARENTING: THE BEST THAT YOU CAN BE

friends. Invariably, Lucy smashes him over the head with the inferiority. If he'd keep his feelings to himself, people wouldn't even notice his inadequacies. People are too busy thinking about themselves anyway! But whenever someone sees himself as a loser, as Charlie Brown does, he expects to fail and behaves in a manner that makes failure more likely and success less likely.

Whereas Charlie Brown's personality showcases negative self-worth, Snoopy provides a grand look at positive feelings of worth. Snoopy sees himself playing the piano well enough to fill concert halls. Confidently, he flexes his muscles while reflecting on his image in a mirror and wonders what the homely dogs are doing. He thinks of himself as a sports 'super-star', knows the 'chicks' can't resist a graceful beagle, successfully fends off any snowball coming in his direction, and thinks of himself as a world-famous hockey player, skating off for the finish. His popularity reaches such a magnitude that his fan mail piles up.

One of the most remarkable characteristics of Snoopy revolves around his ability to make a mistake and bounce back. While playing hockey, he may commit a foul, end up in the penalty box (his dog house) and quip, 'Well, nobody's perfect.'

> The **Peanuts** series provides graphic and powerful images of how those with both positive and negative self-images respond to life. The major task of a parent revolves around helping a child develop the positive characteristics showcased in Snoopy, and fewer of the negative traits manifested in Charlie Brown. A parent's success or failure at this will, to a large degree, determine a child's eventual success or failure in life.

What is self-worth?

Self-worth is the centre of emotional and mental health. Many definitions of self-worth have been given, but a simple one that spells it out clearly is how positive and loving one feels towards oneself. Nathaniel Branden, a pioneer in the field of understanding self-worth (or self-esteem), says: 'Self-esteem is the experience of being competent to cope with the basic challenges of life and of being worthy of happiness.' 'Self-respect,' according to Dr Branden, 'is confidence in our right to be happy; confidence that achievement, success, friendship, respect, love, and fulfilment are appropriate to us.' [1]

It's up to you as a parent to instil these traits in your child. If you successfully handle this assignment, the end result will be an

Chapter 1 // Help your child develop positive self-worth

emotionally healthy child who can handle almost any challenge successfully, a child with more Snoopy traits. If you neglect or fail at this task, your child will more likely respond to life as Charlie Brown does – with shaky self-confidence and difficulty controlling his life.

> Possessing self-worth means your child can accept his weaknesses along with his strengths. Self-worth allows your child to feel equal to others – not better than others, as pride does. Lucy manifests pride when she proudly announces, 'I'm smarter than you.'

How solid are your child's feelings of worth: or your own? If either of you has fragile or low feelings of worth, it will make you susceptible to endless emotional trauma as the years drag by. Energy and maturity are needed to manage the parent role. It is emotional and mental stability that produces parenting confidence, strength and happiness. When one or both are unhealthy there is a strong probability that the relationship between parent and child will be damaged.

The way a child views himself forms the basis on which he will make choices and react to situations for the rest of his life. It determines the values he will live by and the goals he'll pursue, and forms the basis of his belief system. A child's response to life events is, to a large extent, shaped by what he thinks about himself. Remember: self-image is not what a person actually is. Ninety percent of the self-image revolves around what we think others think of us. We allow our self-worth to be determined by others!

Sometimes a child's perception of himself gets distorted. A child can be loved by his parents and friends and still not love himself. He could be voted the most popular student at school and still feel worthless due to prior experiences which have negatively impacted his self-image. Even honours and awards given by others cannot dislodge the firmly embedded feelings of worthlessness, because they originate within. Success in the eyes of friends does not necessarily spell success inside.

The self-concept your child has, then, is formed from a combination of all past experiences – including his relationships with others, and his successes and failures in life. This formulates what he thinks others think about him. Building self-worth doesn't stand alone, since it is vitally connected with how a parent communicates, disciplines, sets limits and trains a child. It is the determining factor in a child's character and spiritual development.

PARENTING: THE BEST THAT YOU CAN BE

Why love isn't enough

Loving a child is not enough. A child must feel acceptance – that he occupies a valuable position in your family. This needs to be felt whether or not he accomplishes anything great in life. A child is not capable of experiencing or returning love until he first learns to respect himself. The single most important determinant of a child's self-worth between the ages of 1 and 12 is his perception of how much his parents value him.

Keep in mind three factors when evaluating self-worth:

1. Self-worth is learned.
A child is not born feeling good about himself, although tendencies towards either positive or negative feelings about oneself may be inherent. Rather, self-worth is a learned response to the combination of life's experiences. It generally stems from a child's daily interactions with those around him. Through the total input of life's experiences, then, a child develops either positive or negative feelings of worth.

Just as Charlie Brown developed a belief in his inferiority, so can a child. Charlie Brown learned that drinking fountains target and drench him, that no one likes him, and that he's a miserable flop on the pitcher's mound. Such experiences are firmly planted in his brain because they happen repeatedly. Failure is the name of the game for him. Experience upon experience teaches him he cannot measure up to others.

Just as Charlie Brown learned to be down-in-the-mouth, so a child learns negative or positive feelings of worth. The more positive experiences you provide and the more positive feedback your child receives from you, the greater the chance he will learn that he is a person of worth and value.

Chapter 1 // Help your child develop positive self-worth

2. Self-worth can be earned.
Questions about performance and ability play a big part in the development of self-worth. Tasks done well foster feelings of adequacy.

Spoken or unspoken, 'How am I doing?' lurks in the subconscious of every child's mind. Regardless of how well a child is performing a task, parents often subtly convey that, if he had tried harder, he could have done better. When a parent feels that way about a child, it comes across verbally as well as non-verbally. Children are adept at picking up clues revealing such thinking.

Productivity, performance and creativity promote feelings of worth. A child will never like himself if he thinks he can't do anything well. Therefore, every child needs a 'speciality' – a skill or ability through which he (or she) can earn self-worth. By developing skills and abilities, a child can enhance his sense of worth. This aspect of self-respect can be reinforced through comments such as, 'You're showing real talent in drawing,' or, 'You are excelling in chemistry,' or, 'You are doing well in computer skills.'

3. Self-worth must be experienced.
You can repeatedly tell your child, 'I love you. I think you are great.' But if your child doesn't feel loved and accepted, words will not convince him, no matter how many times they are repeated. You can talk all you want about love: 'Of course we love you. We think you're wonderful.' But if your actions don't match your words, your child will see right through you.

A child senses when his parents don't really value him, and he concludes, 'You say you love me, but you only say that because you have to. I know you aren't really proud of me. I'm not really important to you. Somehow I've disappointed you. I haven't turned out the way you wanted me to.'

A child is convinced of this every time someone asks him a question and you answer for him, when you brief him on what and what not to say before he goes to a friend's house. He gets the point through other subtle messages that reinforce the thought that he might make you look bad. Through this and other subtle messages picked up, his sense of whether you really 'like' and value him is finalised.

Self-respect, then, is a positive attitude towards oneself gained by learning, earning and experiencing.

PARENTING: THE BEST THAT YOU CAN BE

Where does self-worth come from?

The roots of self-worth begin early in life as trust develops. Trust develops in the first eighteen months of life as an infant lies in the arms of a loving mother and recognises safety. Over time Mum becomes synonymous with safety and comfort. Trust comes when the baby feels Dad's strong arms around him. He learns over time that Dad will be there when needed. Trust is also learned as Mum nurses the infant and hunger pangs are satisfied. Trust continues to build when soiled nappies are changed and the baby is gently laid in his cot and covered with a soft blanket.

The child who does not develop this trust grows up an untrusting, totally self-reliant, distant person who seeks to control the world and his relationships. He thinks others can't be trusted, just as his caregivers could not be trusted. Trust must be developed during this time as it is foundational to self-worth.

As the baby gets older, he experiences a sense of accomplishment as he masters rolling over and getting things into his mouth. These early experiences of success give a baby a 'can do' attitude. Every time he falls down when learning to walk, but tries again and succeeds, he gains a sense of accomplishment that bolsters developing self-worth. He also formulates thoughts about worth based on interactions with those around. By age 3 or 4, a child has already formed many conclusions; what he can accomplish and what he is worth. Such thoughts begin to crystallise.

The early teen years, 13 to 15, might be described as the most difficult thirty-six months of teen life. This is when inferiority and self-doubt reach an all-time high. This child's worth hangs on whether a certain group accepts him (and such groups can be notoriously fickle). Even minor evidence of rejection takes on major significance to youngsters who already feel like failures. The impact of having no one to sit with on a school-sponsored bus trip, not having an invitation to an important school event, being laughed at by a 'teaser', waking up to a shiny new pimple, or falling down in front of someone special – all take on larger-than-life proportions.

Furthermore, members of this age group can be brutal to one another, attacking and slashing one another's self-worth in such a vicious manner that the victim may never recover. Junior-high years are critical to the development of healthy self-worth. It isn't uncommon to see a bright-eyed, happy youngster enter junior high school and emerge three years later broken and

20

Chapter 1 // Help your child develop positive self-worth

discouraged. Such children leave junior high hating their bodies, feeling they have no appeal to the opposite sex, and wishing they'd never been born. Teens desperately need help during this critical period of intensive self-doubt. One study says that 80% of children enter first grade feeling good about themselves. By the fifth grade only 20% do. And just 5% of high-school seniors feel good about themselves.

The teenager brings with him all the experiences and feelings accumulated from the years that have gone before. Now he begins evaluating himself against these past experiences.

During childhood the self-concept is not so firmly fixed, and can be moulded, encouraged and changed more easily: but during adolescence the self-concept is less flexible. Previous judgements become more fixed. Labels like the 'class clown', the 'shy one', the 'big mouth', the 'teaser', the 'nerd', the 'sports nut', or the 'wallflower' become more fixed.

Once an evaluation is accepted as valid, change becomes difficult. Parents, teachers, counsellors and friends may attempt to help improve this child's self-worth, only to have their efforts rejected. The reason is simple: once a child begins to think of himself as a 'slow learner' or whatever, he will put up steel-like resistance to prove every other label wrong. The results of this belief system are found, for example, in the beautiful girl who believes she is ugly because she grew up with the idea that she is ugly. She rejects any information contrary to her fixed ideas about herself.

Wounded spirits

During a seminar, I addressed reasons why parents might reject a child. One parent abruptly interrupted, 'Why talk about rejecting a child? I don't know any parents who have rejected their child.' With equal fervour a social worker from the other side of the room responded, 'Every day of my life I deal with battered and abused children. There is a sick world out there, and many parents are rejecting their kids for reasons they may not fully understand themselves.'

Let's take a look at some of the sources of parental rejection which result in wounded spirits: [2]

NEGLECT.

Neglect is a form of abuse by parents who are too busy or immature to meet the demands of young children. Divorce often takes such a heavy emotional toll on the adult that there is little left to give to a youngster. Neglect of children in the dizzying pace of today's hectic world is most likely the major underlying problem plaguing children today.

Chronic neglect, especially during the first two years of life, can be devastating both psychologically and neurologically. In order to develop normally, the brain needs stimulation from the outside world. When a child is mistreated, ignored, left alone or shuffled from one caregiver to another, it takes a terrible toll on emotional stability. The greater the neglect, the greater the damage.

PARENTING: THE BEST THAT YOU CAN BE

UNWANTED OR UNPLANNED CHILDREN.

Many couples today engage in sex prior to marriage and are totally unprepared for reality when the home pregnancy kit confirms their fears. Their emotions orbit as they face grave decisions about possible marriage, shattered educational dreams, abortion, adoption and financial responsibility. Should the father fail to accept responsibility for the child, the rejection felt by the mother often passes to the child. By five and a half months, the fallout engulfs babies in the womb. By then they can experience both positive and negative emotions from the mother as if they were their own emotions. The baby in the womb is affected by any medication ingested or even the rush of adrenaline. This is also true when the father is abusive to the mother. The helpless unborn child absorbs the mother's anxieties, fears and apprehensions about bringing her baby into the world with so much uncertainty.

Following birth, the unmarried woman often struggles to express the same approval and admiration of her child that she could have if she were married and welcoming her child into a home with two parents. Some may think it inconceivable that an infant can perceive such feelings immediately after birth. Yet infants can perceive feelings long before they can express them in words. An unwanted child understands he is an inconvenience. Such a child is wounded repeatedly each time the story unfolds surrounding his birth without two parents.

DIFFICULT BIRTHS.

Difficult or life-threatening births often form the roots of rage, since the child perceives that someone may be trying to kill or harm him. Not all difficult births are preventable, but issues of rejection can still stem from birth trauma.

LACK OF BONDING TIME.

The first two to four hours are needed for Mother (and ideally Father) to bond with their newborn. Each newborn searches for the eyes of parents to reflect back the adoration and love so badly needed to thrive. Unless the child experiences the eye, voice and touch bonding, along with the caring so desperately needed during the first critical hours, he may always feel detached from his family. It is during this time that the child establishes his sense of identity and connection to his mother and father. Siblings and grandparents should also have a place in this bonding experience.

HARSH TREATMENT.

After birth all five senses gather information. Before a baby can understand the spoken word, he is capable of interpreting rejection. When a child is handled roughly or

Chapter 1 // Help your child develop positive self-worth

experiences physical pain, it is recorded in his memory bank. Angry or frightened faces, the taste or smell of unpleasant substances – all are recorded. Even a parental look of disappointment or disgust can be interpreted by a sensitive child as meaning that he is unwanted. He concludes: 'I made another mistake. I'm no good.' Scoldings, put-downs and physical or verbal abuse are automatically stored to be recalled later and destroy the roots of self-worth.

When the child's primary caregivers are not meeting the child's needs, the child will react by withdrawing, thumb-sucking, needing his blanket, dummy or bottle, fussing, crying or demanding that those needs be met. Fear and rejection are adopted as defensive behaviours. Those damaged in the first eighteen months of life, when trust should be developed, will have difficulty trusting or accepting themselves and others.

ADOPTION.

Even though they are adored by their adoptive parents, adopted children often feel rejected by their birth parents. Feelings of emptiness and disconnectedness often haunt adoptees. In the back of their mind they always wonder, 'Why did my parents give me away? What's wrong with me that they gave me away?' Such questions will arise again when the children begin searching for their biological parents.

BUSYNESS.

Financial pressures, frequent moves and high expectations can also be root causes for parental rejection. Overwork, low pay and desperation exact a terrible toll as parents struggle to make sense of crammed calendars, hectic homes, starved marriages and splintered dreams. Rejection can also be caused by loving parents who become too busy or preoccupied to meet the child's need for attention and approval.

When feelings of rejection surface, they flood the victim with feelings of worthlessness. Once such feelings solidify, rejection forms the foundation of the child's belief system, which is well established by the age of 8. Now life is viewed through a filter of rejection. Everywhere he looks, rejection lurks. Feelings of worthlessness rob him of the happiness, friendship, love and success he could enjoy.

Behaviour modification techniques can change a child's behaviour, but not necessarily the feelings and thoughts resulting from early damage. Adults who have been damaged in the past can find healing only by examining their painful past and leaving it with God to bring about healing.

23

PARENTING: THE BEST THAT YOU CAN BE

PARENTAL FIGHTING.

When parental fighting spins around them, children assume they are part of it or in some way caused it. Screaming matches, threats, obscenities, demeaning accusations, throwing things – all make indelible impressions upon young minds. The same goes for pushing, slapping or hitting. When children observe this, it might as well be happening to them. The child feels a responsibility to fix the situation or protect the parent receiving the abuse. Since it is impossible for a child to solve adult problems, he bears the pain, guilt, shame and rejection that accompany parental disputes.

INCONSISTENT DISCIPLINE.

Parents who mete out discipline based on their mood of the moment produce insecurity and multiple anxieties within a child. A child's sense of security is based to a large degree on a predictable pattern of living. When a child experiences inconsistent discipline, his security is threatened.

The first emotional task a child tackles is trust. But trust can only develop in an atmosphere of predictability. When some behaviour is allowed one day but not the next, the child becomes confused and anxious. A child becomes adept at reading the facial expressions, tones of voice and attitudes of a parent. Before a parent explodes in anger, children sense tension in the air. Fear and distrust over what they have said or done to cause such rage haunts them. As a result, some children grow up with such paralysing fear that they are unable to make decisions.

The message received from inconsistent discipline is, 'I can't do anything right.' Rather than try, the child retreats to the safety of his own world. The child learns that he can never measure up and cannot depend on Mum or Dad.

DRUG AND ALCOHOL ADDICTION.

If an addict is forced to choose between his drug and his child, the addiction almost always wins. Addictions consume the addict's time and attention.

Whatever the addictive substance, the brain is numbed so the parent is unavailable to give the nurture and affection the child so desperately needs. It doesn't take the child long to work out that his parent prefers his addiction to him. The parent who is high on drugs or stupefied by alcohol cannot meet the emotional needs of a child. And the entire family find themselves dancing around the addict. The child then takes on the responsibility of 'fixing' or helping his parent. The child is robbed of the innocence and delight of childhood.

DIVORCE.

Since a major portion of a child's security and worth comes from a loving and healthy relationship between his mother and father, divorce will always have a damaging effect on children. To a large degree, a child of divorcing parents goes through the same stages of grief that he would if a parent had died. The child experiences shock, depression, denial, anger, fear and a haunting obsession that he might be responsible.

Toddlers (2 to 4 years of age) frequently regress to more baby-like behaviour: needing nappies, wanting to be fed. They tend to suffer from irritability, whining, crying, fearfulness, sleep problems, confusion, aggressiveness and tantrums. This age group is the one most seriously affected by divorce.

Young children (ages 5 to 8) also regress in their behaviour to bed-wetting, loss of sleep, nail-biting, irrational fears of being abandoned and a deep sense of sadness. One study showed that 25 to 50% of this age group continued having severe symptoms and yearned for their fathers. Some believe this to be the most critical period for a child to experience divorce.

Older children (ages 9 to 12) experience, primarily, anger – usually taken out on others outside the family. Rejection of parental values is most likely to occur now. The spiritual development comes into play: 'I don't want anything to do with a religion that can't help my parents solve their problems.'

Teenagers seem less affected, probably because they can understand the reasons for the divorce. They, too, are deeply traumatised, however. The more removed the teen is from the divorce proceedings, the better he can handle the situation.

When the divorce is hotly contested, as in custody battles, and where children are used as go-betweens, the effects can be worse. The child's normal coping capacity is more seriously impaired. The effects of divorce on children are not always short-lived. Studies show that 37% of all

PARENTING: THE BEST THAT YOU CAN BE

children whose parents divorced suffered depression even five years later. Chronic and pronounced unhappiness, sexual promiscuity, drug abuse, petty stealing, alcoholism, acts of breaking and entering, poor learning, intense anger, apathy, restlessness, and a sense of intense and unresolved needs now manifest themselves. Another 29% made appropriate developmental progress, but manifested continued symptoms of sadness and resentment towards one or both parents.[3]

The experts agree that children need three to four years to start healing after a divorce. This means that, if a child is 4 when the divorce occurs, he will be 7 or 8 before the effects subside – almost half of his life lived in the awful shadow and aftermath of divorce: another devastating blow to self-respect.

REMARRIAGE.

Children often feel abandoned with divorce but feelings of rejection may actually intensify when remarriage occurs. They often feel their parent has formed an alliance with a stranger. Most children, even those from very troubled homes, would go to almost any length to get their divorced parents together again. Most of them share a common fantasy – that their parents will reunite. This fantasy often lives on for years. Often misbehaviour is geared towards making a step-parent miserable enough to leave, making it possible for the children's biological parents to get back together again.

DYSFUNCTIONAL PARENTS.

Studies reveal that the emotional pain experienced by parents gets passed on to their children through their DNA.[4,5] Whatever damage the parents suffered, their child also receives. Sometimes parents reject a child, not because of something the child has done,

Chapter 1 // Help your child develop positive self-worth

but because they were rejected during their developing years. Clearly it has to do with their own emotional pain. Their inability to love and accept their child comes as a by-product of never being accepted themselves. Parents must possess feelings of worth before they can give them away.

The results of long-term rejection are manifested through extreme hostility, rage, aggression, stress, depression, insecurity and anxiety. Less obvious symptoms include inhibitions, indifference, quietness, withdrawal and extreme submissiveness.

> **In the book Belonging,[6]** author Dr Ron Rockey tells how he reacted to his own rejection with absolute rage. He expressed his rage in overt ways even as a child. He had burned down his family's garage by the time he was 5, and shot flaming arrows into the sides of passing trucks. With his friends, he played cops and robbers in a stone quarry with live ammunition flying overhead. The more dangerous the activity, the more thrilling it was.
>
> He sabotaged academic success by quitting school in the ninth grade. A judge forced him to decide between reform school and enlisting in the armed forces. Later, while serving in the pastoral ministry, the self-admitted arrogant air he created to cover his feelings of inadequacy turned people off. People saw him as a super-controlling person on a big-time ego trip who resisted everybody for the purpose of being obstinate.

Children damaged before the age of 8 cease their emotional maturing near the age at which the damage took place. Such children grow up to be physical adults but remain emotional dwarfs who expect everyone to meet their needs. They expect life to centre on them because no one else matters. Meals must be served at their command and schedules bent to revolve around them. They can display childish temper tantrums any time, anywhere. They expect everyone else to be responsible but show no responsibility themselves.

Those who experienced severe rejection in childhood have instant access to that pain. Their memory is supercharged with the emotion felt at the time it was made. Even repressed memories play a dramatic part in current choices and behaviour.

Beauty and the best

In addition to the sources of parental rejection, society has created a system of false values that effectively adds to the destruction of self-worth. Understanding these destructive forces gives us ammunition to help a child through the difficult formative years.

PHYSICAL APPEARANCE.

If your child was born attractive, he or she has a distinct advantage. Society values attractiveness in both boys and girls. By age 3 or 4, a child has already learned what attractiveness can do for her. The adorable child has learned that people respond favourably to her. People smile and make comments about 'how beautiful' or 'cute' she is and make a fuss over her. The unattractive child beside her, whether it be sibling or friend, stands hesitantly in the shadows, overlooked.

The media is largely responsible for the impact of body perfection as they parade

PARENTING: THE BEST THAT YOU CAN BE

before us and our young children 'super models', 'hunks', 'playmates', and 'jocks'. Eating disorders and dieting are prevalent today even among children as young as 9 or 10. A study conducted a few years ago revealed that 80% of 9-year-old girls were attempting to diet because they thought they were fat. Even thin youngsters are terrified of getting 'fat'. Such thinking invades the psyche of even young children.

Diana, Princess of Wales, struggled with an eating disorder reflecting her response to what she saw in the mirror. It didn't matter that she was one of the most photographed women in the world or a woman of wealth and popularity. Even Miss Americas are bothered by what they consider physical flaws. Few young women are comfortable with their bodies. To complicate matters, television shows now take women with body and facial problems and perform humongous amounts of surgery on them to turn 'ugly ducklings' into 'breathtakingly beautiful women'. Does anyone track these women to learn how they fare a few months after their transformation?

Body image presents as many problems for boys as for girls. Boys desperately long to be big, powerful and handsome. By age 4, boys flex their muscles in hopes of a 'bump' that will soon grow as big as Dad's. Boys dress like Spiderman and Superman. Even small boys struggle with self-worth problems. Think of a small boy in his classroom being pushed and shoved around, being called 'Shrimp' or 'Peanut'. Imagine how he feels when he's shorter than the girls. Then the captain doesn't choose him for his team, and the opposing team calls out, 'You take him this time. We had him last time!'

Life can be just as difficult for the child who is different from his peer group in some way – who has ears that protrude, wears thick glasses, has acne or pock-marked skin, buck teeth or front teeth with a space between them, who is too tall or too short, too fat or too thin, or who is of a race or religion different from the norm of the group. These kids can be teased until life is unbearable, and each day at school becomes agony.

Some parents feel no responsibility for having an embarrassing feature fixed. One father told me, 'I made it through school in spite of my buck teeth, and my kid can too!' He may have made it through school, but it is tougher now. We don't deliberately want our kids to suffer. If the feature is 'fixable' and you can possibly afford it, it should be fixed to spare your child unnecessary trauma.

Chapter 1 // Help your child develop positive self-worth

> **Pressure from bullying and taunting can be severe enough to make some consider suicide. Dr James Dobson in Bringing Up Boys [7] tells of a 12-year-old who considered suicide because his ears stuck out. His mother found him crying one night in his room. After some gentle probing she learned that because of the taunting he had received at school he wanted to end his life. He'd heard that toothpaste could be harmful when swallowed, so he considered eating an entire tube to end it all. This boy was not from a dysfunctional family with multiple problems. He was a good student who made better-than-average grades. His parents eventually learned that when he passed a 'jock' in the school hallway, this jock would put his hands behind his ears, forcing them out and calling him names. As a result this boy felt like the ugliest boy in school.**
>
> **You may think this boy was overreacting or that he'd get over it and go on to laugh at the way things were. But never underestimate the power such distress can have on a child. What looks like no big deal to us can have devastating results for a youngster. And never take threats of suicide lightly, especially from a teenager.**

Don't assume that bullying can't happen because your child attends a 'Christian school'.

Especially guard a teen as he enters junior high. At 13 and 14, youngsters are highly vulnerable to peer pressure. If they make it through junior high with their self-worth intact, they are likely to be able to handle almost anything.

The consensus of opinion used to be that most kids are basically happy and carefree. Yet according to Dr Archibald Hart,[8] author and psychologist, signs of serious depression show up in children as young as 5. These symptoms include lethargy – dreading getting out of bed in the morning, moping around the house, no interest in activities previously enjoyed. Other warning signs include sleep disturbances, stomach complaints, anger, hostility and rage.

Once you become aware of symptoms that signal depression, help your child identify his feelings and put them into words. Learn 'empathetic listening' (explained in the next chapter). Be available to listen. Take the time. In empathetic listening you eliminate judging, belittling or telling the child what to do once he opens up. Simply being heard goes a long way in a child's world. Through this type of listening, you'll gain the information that will direct you to the root cause of the depression.

Who affects self-worth?

Parents usually have the strongest impact on a child, but they aren't the only ones who affect self-respect. Anyone spending long periods of time with the child contributes to shaping his self-image. This person may be a relative, neighbour, baby-sitter, day-care provider or sibling. Teachers also have a marked influence over a child because of the long hours spent under their tutelage. The child is not as dependent on these people as he is on parents for emotional needs. But when a child continuously interacts with any one person, that person becomes an intimate part of his life and affects self-respect.

PARENTING: THE BEST THAT YOU CAN BE

Once a child begins school, the horizons for self-worth widen. Until now he has accepted family values. But now the traits valued by peers take precedence. He'll learn that boys value sports, muscles, adventure and bravery, while girls place more value on appearance and personality. Whether or not he feels he possesses these qualities affects how he feels about himself.

Jason, who is tall, well co-ordinated and good at sports, feels differently about himself than Josh, who is small for his age, introverted and less co-ordinated. Josh thinks he lacks the traits his peers want and value. As a result he concludes that he's not worth much. Because of Jason's skills, his peers vie to have him on their team. His parents and teammates take pride in his achievements. Almost without effort, Jason ends up feeling better about himself than Josh.

A child reacts emotionally to his growth, size, appearance, strength, intelligence, friendliness, skills, and handicaps. He draws conclusions about himself, partly by measuring himself against his peers and partly from how his peers respond to him. Each conclusion adds to or subtracts from his feelings of worth. Some successes carry more weight if he personally feels they are important. An early-teen boy may excel at playing the violin, but, if he is a failure at football, even being first fiddle in the orchestra will not make up for it since his friends won't value it. Every activity a child participates in gives him more information about who he is and what he's worth. Clubs, sports, church groups, schools and jobs all add to his identity bank.

The more acceptance, affirmation and value he has collected from his family, the more rejection he can withstand from those outside the family.

Although you as a parent are not totally responsible for your child's self-concept, you are a major player. How you relate to your child during the early years at home sets the stage for his later success or failure in life.

30

Chapter 1 // Help your child develop positive self-worth

Symptoms of rejection

Is it possible for a parent to tell when a child has self-worth problems? Yes. When a child suffers from low self-worth, failure and criticism dominate his emotions. Self-reproach for not measuring up causes him to justify his existence by creating arguments for his own defence. Fear and anxiety exhaust him emotionally and drain him physically.

Some of the symptoms evidenced in low self-worth would include: a lack of decision-making ability; withdrawal or retreat into a fantasy world; repeated, deliberate misbehaviour; abnormal attempts to please; habitual crying and signs of tension like nail-biting, head-banging and stuttering. It also includes things like putting himself and others down, calling others names, bullying and bragging. Certain physical characteristics such as compulsive eating and obesity, a careless, sagging posture and sloppy appearance, and a sad face and eyes are also symptoms that indicate self-image problems.

Before leaping to conclusions, remember as you take an inventory that normal behaviour varies widely. Don't panic if your child displays a symptom or two occasionally. Look, instead, for patterns of consistency over a period of time. This list is not exhaustive, but designed to help identify tendencies. If your child displays several characteristics repeatedly over a period of time, look for methods to improve his self-image.

The rejected child

If you have determined that your child suffers from rejection at home, school or anywhere else, it is time to act. Tearful episodes, stomach aches and complaints that 'The kids don't like me' signal problems that should be tackled at once. Trying to persuade your child that he shouldn't feel that way or scolding him for his feelings are a big mistake. Such 'feeling stoppers' tell the child that his feelings are not safe with you. Instead, encourage your child to express hurt feelings. Through empathetic listening (taught in the next chapter) you will be able to seek a solution that will help your child develop the necessary coping skills so he can receive the acceptance he so desperately needs from his peers.

Teach your child how to make friends. To help him learn, invite a friend to spend time at your home or go on a picnic with your family. Such experiences teach necessary social skills and encourage the development of a genuine friendship. Teach him to cope, rather than mope.

PARENTING: THE BEST THAT YOU CAN BE

Note: the worse a child's behaviour, the greater his cry for approval. The more your child misbehaves – the more trying, withdrawn or obnoxious he acts – the more starved he is for attention and acceptance. The greater the defences, withdrawal, over-sensitivity or misbehaviour, the greater the need. Often such aggravating behaviours cause parents and teachers to dish out more punishment, and negative comments are directed towards the one starving for love and reassurance. The very defences the child erects lessen the possibility of winning the affection and acceptance he craves. Parent and child are thus caught in a vicious cycle. Most defences can be traced to a child's hidden conviction that he is bad, unworthy, inadequate and unlovable.

Six sure-fire strategies for building self-worth

The self-worth of a child can be nurtured and encouraged as well as changed. No child is so badly damaged that improvements cannot be noted – sometimes in a relatively short time-frame. However, the longer a child lives with a negative picture of himself, the more difficult change becomes. Because of this, positive feelings towards self need to be established early.

Listed here are some strategies for building self-worth. Some are quick and easy to put into effect; others are more long-term. Over the long haul, when employed consistently, each can produce a major positive impact on self-worth.

1. AFFIRM YOUR CHILD DAILY.

Many parents pay more attention to a child when she behaves badly than when she is good. Attention focused on bad behaviour encourages a child who needs attention to be bad to get it! Change your focus from responding to bad behaviour to reinforcing good behaviour. Look for behaviours you can appreciate every morning before your child leaves for school and before she goes to bed at night.

When Susie spells a word correctly, affirm her. When Chris gets a good grade, tell him he did well. When Jonathan ties his shoes, give him a pat on the back. When Kendra plays a song well on the piano, acknowledge her success. Affirm your child for each success and talent displayed. Acknowledge every success, even a small one – for trying hard, helping you, obeying the rules or being kind. Recognise effort and improvement rather than waiting to praise a completed task. Every new task or skill mastered and affirmed boosts self-worth. Children remember positive statements. They can be stored and 'replayed' when needed. Practise affirming your child many times a day.

2. GIVE RESPONSIBILITY AND ALLOW A CHILD TO DO IT ON HIS OWN.

Children need opportunities to help with tasks around the house. Frequently we ask a child to handle some chore and then we take it away because we can do it more quickly and easily. For example, you ask 5-year-old Elizabeth to sweep the kitchen floor. She struggles with the broom. Important tasks beckon from the other end of the house. 'Here, let me finish that,' you say in exasperation as you take the broom. Oops! A

Chapter 1 // Help your child develop positive self-worth

message implying that she can't do things right or fast enough just slipped out. This message chips away at her self-worth.

Children need to learn to complete tasks on their own. It may take them a little longer when they are learning a new task. But their developing self-confidence needs to struggle with solving problems on their own. Never, on a regular basis, do for your child what she should be doing for herself. Break big tasks into a series of easy steps while clearly explaining how the task can be completed. Then give her a chance to complete it. Let her know you believe in her and expect her to do well.

3. TEACH YOUR CHILD TO MAKE GOOD DECISIONS.

There are several ways parents can help a child improve his or her decision-making ability. First, clarify the need for a decision. Ask questions that pinpoint how he sees, hears and feels about the situation: 'I know you're having trouble with maths, Brennan. Can you think of a way to improve your grade? What has your teacher said?' Secondly, brainstorm solutions together: 'Yes, you can study harder or stay after school and have your teacher work with you. A tutor might also be helpful.'

Then ask Brennan to choose the solution that he thinks might work best. Guide him towards considering the consequences of each choice. The best solution will be the one that solves the problem and allows Brennan to end up feeling good about the situation and himself.

Later, review the results of his choice with him. Did it work out well? Did it fail? If so, why? Reviewing the outcome equips him to make better decisions next time. The respect shown for his ability to make decisions and deal with the outcome shows that you value his abilities – another boost to self-worth.

4. EXPRESS LOVE AND ATTENTION NON-VERBALLY.

Non-verbal expressions of attention are as important as affirming your child out loud. Since 55% of what is conveyed in any message is sent through body language, non-verbal expressions of affection just might be more important than what you say out loud. So use this avenue often.

PARENTING: THE BEST THAT YOU CAN BE

Give Roseanne a hug or a loving pat. Send a wink to Cliff with a smile. Hold hands with Morgan when going for a walk. When Zack is sitting near, pull him close. Give a high-five to Dan, a pat on the back to Eric, or a back-rub to Amber. A thumbs-up conveys that you agree with Mary Jo without saying a word. A warm smile to Mona sends approval and unconditional love. Though unspoken, such non-verbal messages send constant reminders of approval and affection: another method of boosting self-worth. You can spend money on music or tennis lessons, but none of them mean much unless they are delivered in a spirit of love. Love and value your child, and your child will flourish!

A volunteer tells of going to work with Mother Teresa in the streets of Calcutta to serve the poorest of the poor. Upon arrival, Mother Teresa began a tour of their children's home. The tour was interrupted when some workers brought in a baby that they had rescued off the streets. It was apparent that the baby would not survive the day. Mother Teresa picked up the baby, handed her to the new volunteer and said, 'We'll finish our tour later. Do not let this baby die without having been loved.'

The volunteer later wrote: 'I held that baby in my arms and I loved her until she died at six o'clock in the evening. I spent the hours humming a Brahms lullaby. And you know, I could feel that baby as tiny and weak as she was, I could feel that baby pressing herself against me.'

Even a dying infant responds to human touch.

5. TEACH YOUR CHILD POSITIVE SELF-TALK.

Experts say that 75% of our daily thinking patterns are negative. Negative thinking works against your child instead of helping him build positive self-worth. Once negative thoughts take hold, they become difficult to change. A child looks to prove what he already thinks about himself. If he thinks others don't like him, he will look for evidence to prove this.

Negative self-talk sounds something like this:
- **I'm so stupid.**
- **I'll never pass that maths test.**
- **I can't do anything right.**

It is important to teach a child to be positive about how he 'talks' to himself. The minute you hear or pick up on this type of thinking, ask the child to stop, erase and replace. Stop the negative statement, erase it from his mind and replace it with a positive one. 'I am a smart person and can learn to do things right.' 'I can study hard and pass that maths test.' 'I can try that task again and do it better.' Whether a child tells himself positive or negative messages plays a tremendous part in shaping what really happens in his life.

6. DEVELOP A SKILL OR ABILITY.

Every child needs to be able to do something well, to have a skill or ability that allows him to shine before others – particularly if he is different from his group; if he is too short, too tall, too fat, too thin, has protruding teeth, wears glasses, has ears that stick out, or is racially or religiously different. Whenever a child is different from the norm, he is likely to get picked on. Being raised by immigrant parents, having a handicapped sibling, financial hardship or medical conditions, or having an alcoholic parent or a parent in prison sets the child up to be picked on. Being called names, made fun of or ridiculed has the potential for wounding the child for life.

A nickname may not appear vicious, but often a child becomes her nickname. This can have devastating effects on self-worth. When a girl is called 'Tank' and sees herself as a 'tank' she will think of herself as odd, different, and deformed. How can she respect or like herself when she sees herself like this? Children are keenly aware of how they rank among their classmates. Who gets the best grades in class? Who is the best artist? Musician? Ball player? Who gets invited to parties and who doesn't? Who receives the most Valentines and who doesn't? Who's the most popular? At the end of any school day, a child who started out feeling happy and confident can return home feeling like a washout and a failure – just from name-calling and peer pressure. Lack of friends, feeling unaccepted, and not being included in social circles are serious problems for children of all ages, but especially during adolescence.

About 50% of America's children have IQ scores below 100, which means they are at high risk of experiencing learning problems. Approximately 22% have an IQ of between 70 and 90, which places them in the 'slow learner' range. This puts the slow learner at high risk of developing serious feelings of inferiority. Unless the self-worth of a slow learner is carefully nurtured, he will proceed through school feeling 'dumb' and thus act 'dumb'. [9]

Academia or the attainment of good grades should be de-emphasised for such children. Although a child needs to be held accountable to do his best, pressure to achieve good grades should be removed. Instead, a child in this category should be encouraged to work with his hands, repair

PARENTING: THE BEST THAT YOU CAN BE

motors, fix broken items, build, hammer, sew, cook, clean and master other skills that can provide a sense of accomplishment, without requiring superior intelligence or academic skills.

Every child has strengths, but, when self-worth is low, the child literally thinks he is drowning in an ocean of inadequacy. Words alone won't work now, because the child won't believe them. This is where you, the parent, come in. You must provide your child with a skill or ability that will help him feel like somebody. By the time your child is 8 years of age, this coping talent or ability should be fairly well established. For example, if Thad is small for his age, and not good at sports, he is going to need help, and now. Being good at sports is one of the most valued traits all through high school. Thad may already feel inadequate and be in desperate need of some skill of which he can be proud.

If he's not good at team sports, he might still be good at individual sports like swimming, tennis or ice skating. Don't just give him music lessons and hope for the best! Music can help him in the long term, but he needs something to do well now. Think of martial arts like karate. Such sports are not methods of hurting, destroying or maiming others. Their main purpose is to sharpen judgement and improve self-control, self-confidence and self-discipline. Taekwondo promotes courtesy, integrity, perseverance, self-control and spirit.

Once Thad earns his black belt, who among his peers would call him 'Shrimp'? Regardless of his size, feelings of inferiority no longer plague him. He now possesses the confidence and self-control to take care of himself in any situation. He'll receive a measure of respect wherever he goes.

Martial arts is only one suggestion. The skill or ability a child needs could be developed around art, writing or rock collecting. Will his peers still call him names and make fun of him? They may from time to time. But now there's something inside that fights back. It says, 'That's OK. Go ahead and make fun of me, but I can do something you can't do.' Feelings of inadequacy no longer crush or paralyse him. Now he has the capacity to compensate for his inability to measure up.

All parents should carefully assess their child's strengths and abilities. Select one that holds the greatest

Chapter 1 // Help your child develop positive self-worth

potential for success. Then see that your child has every opportunity to advance in it – reward and push till he's good at it. Should you discover that he cannot hack it, you can always back up and go down another path. Remember, your child does not yet have the maturity to understand what you are trying to help him accomplish. See that he stays with something until he succeeds and enjoys it. This can be a child's greatest weapon against inferiority.

Where it all begins

Your child has the best chance for a strong sense of worth when you possess healthy feelings of worth – when you model it in day-to-day life. You serve as a role model for your child, who is quick to sense if you suffer from feelings of inferiority. If you suffer from low self-worth, it will contaminate your offspring like a virus. As your child observes your Charlie Brown responses to life, he'll subconsciously think, 'Mum and Dad don't feel good about themselves. They don't think they are worth much. So I must not be worth much either.' Low self-worth in a parent, then, almost predisposes a child to accept the same distorted concepts, values and assumptions generated from his parent's inadequacies.

Furthermore, low self-worth often passes from generation to generation – from great-grandparent to grandparent, from parent to child, in a chain reaction. Each generation increases the severity of the malady and those who suffer. Case histories document that suicidal tendencies follow family lines. Unless parents take effective measures to break the vicious spiral, their own low self-worth may cripple even the unborn.

The better we understand the all-encompassing effects of low self-worth, the more we can comprehend that it is the underlying cause of most social problems – alcoholism, suicide, drug addiction, out-of-wedlock pregnancy and crime. Building positive feelings of worth in ourselves and our children is the only way out of these disastrous dilemmas.

You can do it!

Is the atmosphere of your home conducive to building or destroying self-worth? Have you met your child's needs for respect and acceptance today? Can you respect your child for what she is, or must something great be produced before she can win your approval? Must she make you proud before you can accept her? In all the years to come, how will she remember your contributions to her self-worth?

PARENTING: THE BEST THAT YOU CAN BE

A defective self-concept can be reprogrammed, but it remains infinitely easier to build healthy feelings of worth from the beginning rather than trying to repair it later on. Self-worth problems can be repaired. God gives us the power to carry out his purpose as we behold Him – through His Word.

Philippians 4:13 (NIV) promises, 'I can do everything through him who gives me strength.'

Happiness is feeling good about yourself. Self-respect remains the greatest gift you can give your child. The word 'love' can now be profoundly understood. It is a firm foundation for happiness.

Footnotes

[1] Nathaniel Branden, 'What Self-Esteem Is and Is Not', *http://www.nathanielbranden.com/catalog/articles_essays/what_self_esteem.html*

[2] Ron and Nancy Rockey with Kay Kuzma, **Belonging.**

[3] Nancy Van Pelt, **From This Day Forward** (Hagerstown, MD, Review and Herald Publishing), pp. 68, 69.

[4] *https://www.theguardian.com/science/2015/aug/21/study-of-holocaust-surivors-finds-trauma-passed-on-to-childrens-genes*

[5] *http://peterfelix.tripod.com/home/Epigenetic_TTT2.pdf*

[6] **Belonging.**

[7] Dr James Dobson, **Bringing Up Boys** (Wheaton, IL, Tyndale House, 2001), p. 40.

[8] Archibald Hart, **Stress and Your Child** (Nashville, Thomas Nelson/Word).

[9] Dr James Dobson, **Hide or Seek** (Grand Rapids, MI, Fleming H. Revell), p. 90.

CHAPTER 2

Communication is the key

Good parent-child relationships depend on a number of important elements, of which successful communication is certainly near the top of the list: for, as an article published by the Child Development Institute (USA) states: 'Whether you are parenting a toddler or a teenager, good communication is the key to building self-esteem as well as mutual respect.' [1]

The benefits of open and respectful communication styles in the home are far-reaching, as outlined by Kristin Zolten and Nicholas Long (Department of Pediatrics, University of Arkansas for Medical Sciences): 'Parents who communicate effectively with their children are more likely to have children who are willing to do what they are told.' In addition to which, 'Such children know what to expect from their parents, and once children know what is expected of them, they are more likely to live up to these expectations. They are also more likely to feel secure in their position in the family, and are thus more likely to be co-operative.' [2]

With this in mind let us have a look at how we can enhance our own family communication processes.

Better listening tips

1. MAKE THE TIME.

Parents are so busy earning a living and ensuring that the family functions properly, that they sometimes forget to slow things down enough to listen to the little voices in the family. So many important things jam their daily routines. But nothing should be more important than listening to what goes on in your child's world. This doesn't necessarily mean a formal meeting. Utilise the time you are already together, when pottering in the kitchen or garage, when chauffeuring them to a game, at bedtime, or around the dinner table.

2. ACT INTERESTED AND BE ATTENTIVE.

A child can tell whether he has his parents' interest and attention by their body language and their replies. When a child needs to talk, forget other distractions, including your social media. Give your child

PARENTING: THE BEST THAT YOU CAN BE

focused attention by getting on their eye-level, and maintain eye contact. A cartoon illustrated this when the little girl looked at her father who was reading the paper and said, 'Daddy, you have to listen to me with your eyes as well as your ears.'

3. LISTEN TO THE LITTLE STUFF.

A child will talk if you have proved you will listen. If you listen to the little stuff when they are young, they will more likely talk about the heavy issues like difficult schoolwork, sex and drugs as they get older. Listen non-judgementally and your teen will know he can trust you with the big stuff.

4. LISTEN BETWEEN THE LINES.

Many children want to talk with a parent about the things that really matter, but are afraid or don't know how. Listen between the lines for clues about what your child may be trying to say. Watch the emotion behind the words – especially the intensity of the emotion.

5. ASK FOR OPINIONS.

It's a compliment to be asked for an opinion on something. When you ask for a child's opinion on the small stuff as well as the big stuff and prove you have a listening ear, your child is more likely to enjoy expressing his opinion to you: and you might learn something important.

6. DON'T INTERRUPT.

Interrupting is a rude behaviour you would probably not tolerate from your child. In a national survey conducted on children, more than half said that their parents often didn't give them a chance to explain what they meant when they were talking. Slow it down. Give your child a chance to explain what he means, even when you think you know what he will say. Children have a more limited vocabulary and it takes longer for them to find the right words to express themselves. It may also be difficult to listen respectfully and not interrupt, but respect shown now is respect that will come back to you in all the years to come.

7. ENCOURAGE YOUR CHILD TO TALK.

Some children, by temperament, are naturally more talkative than others. Others need an invitation to start talking. You might begin with, 'Tell me about your day at school,' or, 'What was the most fun thing you did at school today?' A child is more likely to share ideas and feelings when he thinks he is an important member of the family and is valued.

8. AVOID DEAD-END QUESTIONS, LIKE: 'DID YOU HAVE A GOOD DAY AT SCHOOL TODAY?'

Questions that require a yes-or-no or a one-word response lead to dead ends. Instead, rephrase your questions so a child can explain, describe or share ideas that will extend the conversation.

9. EXTEND THE CONVERSATION.

The conversation can be extended by picking up a piece of what your child has said and asking a question about it. Using the child's own wording will strengthen his confidence in his conversational skills and reassure him that he is being listened to.

10. ASK YOUR CHILDREN TO RECALL POSITIVE EVENTS IN THEIR LIVES.

Everyone enjoys talking about his accomplishments. A question like, 'What have you done this week that makes you proud?' or, 'What's the best present you ever received?' gives a child a sense of pride. Kids want to be valued in their families.

Negative in, negative out

'How do I get my son to listen to me? That's what I want to know,' a frustrated father groaned. 'His behaviour is so irritating. I correct him, but it only seems to make things worse.' When the child causes the parent a problem, there are several options to consider. Depending on the situation, the parent might ignore the misbehaviour, use empathetic listening, use natural consequences, punish the child or engage his co-operation. When a child causes his parent a problem, another communication skill is needed. Children often annoy, frustrate and irritate us. They can be thoughtless, inconsiderate, destructive, noisy and demanding. They cause extra work, make us late, pester us when we are tired, or mess up a clean house. Without thinking through the end results, most

PARENTING: THE BEST THAT YOU CAN BE

parents take over the situation and try to force the child to do what they want him to do. Children resent being ordered around, given commands and told what they have to or should do. A 'commanding officer' sounds like this: 'Get your room clean this minute!' 'Get in there and practise the piano now!' 'Clean up this mess now!'

Other parents name-call: 'How stupid can you get, boy? Don't act like a moron!' 'The way you're dressed makes you look like a homeless person!' The child who is repeatedly put down begins to picture himself as stupid, a moron or a homeless person. Eventually he accepts that judgement and tries to live up to it. Feelings of worthlessness that begin in childhood can follow him into adult life and handicap him forever. Still others threaten: 'If you don't do what you're told right now I'll . . .' Or they lecture and moralise: 'If you want me to do nice things for you, then you'd better do a few things around here. You always want me to take you to the shops, take you here, and take you there. Well, then, you need to do a few things for me. Do unto others as you would have them do unto you.' Such communication implies that you don't think he is capable of initiating good behaviour.

Kids also hate constant warnings: 'If you climb on that rock you'll fall.' They also hate the martyr act: 'Stop acting that way or you'll drive me crazy!' They resent being compared: 'You aren't trying hard enough. Lisa caught on right away.' They hate sarcasm: 'You, run for president of your class? That's a good one!' They also hate predictions of failure: 'You've lied to me before. You'll lie to me again.'

We as adults would detest any of these things said to us. A child feels the same way when he hears these words. So how can we get a child to change his behaviour and become more co-operative without damaging his self-worth or leaving him with negative feelings? Is there a better way for parents to talk to a child when the child is causing them a problem? Yes!

Putting your message across effectively

Even though your frustration may reach epic proportions, an 'I-statement' can be effective. In a direct manner, tell your child how his unacceptable behaviour makes you feel. 'You never do what you are supposed to' is a poor way to convey strong feelings of irritation. 'I get upset when I see that your chores are not done and find you playing computer games.' 'I get frustrated when I see lights left on all over the house.' 'I feel irritated when I find you watching TV and your homework isn't done.'

I-statements contain a 'feeling' word that describes how you feel about the annoying behaviour. They do not condemn the child but deal instead with the child's unacceptable behaviour.

Chapter 2 // Communication is the key

THERE ARE THREE PARTS TO AN EFFECTIVE I-STATEMENT:

1. A 'feeling' word describing how the unacceptable behaviour affects you: 'I feel . . .'
2. A non-blameful description of the child's behaviour: '. . . when you . . .' (describe the behaviour)
3. An explanation regarding the tangible effect of that behaviour on you – what you now have to do about it: '. . . because . . .'

The pattern for an I-statement flows like this: 'I feel _____(1) when you _____ (2) because _____ (3).'

I-statements are much more likely to produce positive behaviour changes and reduce the feelings of resistance and rebellion that come with put-downs, name-calling, threats, commands and other negative babble. The child interprets these as a judgement of his worth and a challenge to his independence. I-statements refer only to your feelings (which he can hardly argue with).

Here are more examples of effective I-statements. Notice that they contain no commands and no put-downs. The parent does not tell the child what to do.

Example 1:
Dad is handling an important business call on the phone when a noisy fight breaks out between his children. 'I really get irritated when you make so much noise that I can't hear on the phone.'

Example 2:
Mum goes into a child's bedroom and finds that food left unattended has attracted ants. 'I really get frustrated when you leave food in your room because we have a really big problem with ants. Now I have to call Pest Control to take care of it, which is expensive.'

Example 3:
Dad discovers that his son borrowed an expensive tool to build a fort and the tool is missing. 'I feel very angry when you borrow a tool without permission and don't return it, because I can't finish my project without it.'

Example 4:
Mum finds the kitchen door has been left open, which lets flies in. 'I really get disgusted when I find the door open again because now the house is full of flies. Flies carry a lot of germs.'

PARENTING: THE BEST THAT YOU CAN BE

I-statements bring some startling results. It surprises children to learn how their parents feel about their behaviour. Often they say, 'I didn't know that it bugged you so much,' or, 'I didn't think you really cared if I . . .' or, 'How come you never told me before how you felt about this?' We are all basically selfish in pursuit of our own goals, but children are particularly self-centred and often unaware of how their behaviour affects others. Irresponsibility often turns into responsibility once children understand the impact of their behaviour on others.

Some of you might ask, 'Why should I talk to my child that way when I could tell him once to cut it out and get results?' You would be a winner even if you had to repeat the statement a time or two. How? Because your child chose to change his behaviour in respect for your needs. He is learning to respect the rights and needs of others. Second, and perhaps most importantly, he chose a right course of action without being told what to do. Every time your child makes a wise choice without being told, he moves towards self-control and maturity – your ultimate goal in child training.

Note: I-statements effectively produce co-operation and positive behaviour changes, but that is not their primary purpose. The major reason for using I-statements is to release feelings of irritation before you lose control. Your child may or may not change his behaviour as a result of your I-statement, but you are staying in touch with your feelings and communicating them in a direct way rather than suppressing them. Unattended resentments and irritations can fester and result in explosions that the child neither understands nor is responsible for. The head of steam that builds up over the course of any day can be let off by learning to communicate your irritation in an open and direct method.

More about I-statements:

1. Use them when first irritated. Don't wait till you are angry. Once anger sets in it is too late for an I-statement.
2. Avoid sending a solution or telling your child what to do. Letting him figure out a solution to the problem on his own develops critical thinking abilities.
3. If your child does not respond to your first I-statement – as may often happen when you first begin to use them – send another, rephrased in a new manner, until you are heard.

Chapter 2 // Communication is the key

I-statements are powerful, yet few parents use them. Why? Most are too out of touch with their own feelings. A host of emotions have been cut off due to messages from the past – their own parents telling them which emotions are acceptable and which are not. Since they learned from their parents that it wasn't OK to have certain feelings, they are pushed out of their consciousness. These parents have difficulty recognising any feeling in their child that doesn't appear on their 'acceptable' list.

Others have tried I-statements a time or two and received a 'Tough!' or 'So what? You're always upset!' from a mouthy child going through a rebellious stage. This defensive reaction led to further conflict: and they gave up without giving this skill a chance.

Let's look in on an incident where the parent is irritated because the child didn't return for hours after running an errand that should have taken only about thirty minutes . . .

PARENT:

I really get worried when I send you on an errand that should take only thirty minutes. When you are gone for two hours I get scared something awful has happened to you. I have to make phone calls and go searching for you.

CHILD:

I wasn't gone for two hours and you don't have to worry or go looking for me. I can take care of myself, you know.

Such a response evidences a defensive (and rebellious) pattern of communicating. In order to break out of this destructive, self-defeating pattern, a new strategy is needed. A new I-statement must be sent:

PARENT:

I've got a new problem right now. When I tell you about my feelings and get a response like I just got, I do not feel heard or respected. It would be less than honest of me not to tell you how I feel.

45

PARENTING: THE BEST THAT YOU CAN BE

There is still no guarantee that the defensive child will stop defending himself, but at least there is a possibility. But don't allow your child to force you off track. If you really want to have your feelings recognised, you must continually communicate them directly until you are heard and understood. Don't give up just because you didn't get the desired response. There aren't that many constructive options left.

I-statements communicate more effectively because they place the responsibility with the child to co-operate. Through an I-statement he can learn responsibility for his own behaviour. I-statements tell the child that you trust him to handle the situation constructively and to respect your needs.

Over a period of time, I-statements can do more to encourage a child to co-operate – without damaging self-worth or hurting a relationship – than all the rewards, punishments, or nagging most parents have unsuccessfully used. Before you toss this one aside, try it consistently for two weeks!

When communication breaks down

Genuine communication with your child doesn't necessarily mean a rehash of daily events. It does imply daily pleasant association. Some parents feel that they have lost communication with their children because there isn't endless chatter between them. Endless chatter may be a cover-up for deep-seated problems. Genuine communication has taken place if you are in touch with your child and are increasing your ability to accept him as an individual with rights, needs and values of his own.

If, however, communication has broken down with a child, it is up to you to do something about it. The responsibility for repairing communication lines rests squarely on the shoulders of the parent. It hardly matters what the child did to initiate the breach. Find a way of reaching that child, remembering that actions often speak louder than words.

Footnotes

[1] *https://childdevelopmentinfo.com/how-to-be-a-parent/communication/*

[2] *http://www.parenting-ed.org/handouts/communication-parent%20to%20child.pdf*

CHAPTER 3

Odedience: Developing your strategies

> 'Children, obey your parents in the Lord, for this is right.' Ephesians 6:1, NIV

> 'The child that never learns to obey his parents in the home will not obey God or man out of the home.' Josh Billings

One thing that most parents hope for, and work towards, is having obedient children. This is a noble objective but not an easy task. In fact, for most parents, instilling obedience in their children often constitutes a major portion of their daily parent-child interaction. The task of encouraging obedience from our children often starts early and persists through much of the day.

For this reason we need to develop clear and workable strategies that will make this important responsibility as easy and rewarding as possible – for both parent and child. Here are six tried and tested ones that you might want to consider.

Strategy 1: Discipline without anger

Many parents say their biggest challenge is staying calm when their children misbehave, especially when the behaviour challenges their authority and is openly defiant. If you are a parent with a babe in arms, you have yet to see the day when your child will be cheeky, sarcastic, strong-willed and possibly even defiant. Prepare yourself. That day will come. And, when it occurs, you need to keep your cool.

James Dobson tells of a family on vacation. The miles mounted, and so did the father's fury while his two sons bickered, whined, griped, grumbled and fussed in the back seat. Finally the father's fuse was finished. Jerking the car over to the side of the road, the father yanked both boys outside. 'I can't take it any longer!' he screamed in anger. After spanking them both, he shoved them back into the car with a stern warning: 'If I hear a peep from either of you for thirty minutes I'll give you some more of what you just had.'

PARENTING: THE BEST THAT YOU CAN BE

The boys got the message and sat mute. Exactly thirty minutes later, the older brother peeped, 'Is it OK to talk now?' The father barked, 'What do you need to say?' 'Well, when you spanked us back there, my shoe fell off.' When you let anger fly, 'shoes' have a way of 'falling off'. Unchecked anger inevitably boomerangs to bite you.

Anger is a basic human emotion, but 'blowing your top' over your child's behaviour only makes a bad situation worse. Notice that the word 'anger' is only one letter away from 'danger'. Some parents reluctantly admit to yelling, swearing, throwing things, and kicking or even hitting their child – using their child as a punch bag. What does a child learn from such behaviour? To yell, swear, throw things, and kick and hit others.

You cannot discipline effectively until you get your anger under control. Here's a plan for staying calm when disciplining a child: effective training can only take place when anger is under control.

1. RECOGNISE TRIGGERS.

Kids are geniuses at recognising when and how to push our buttons. Certain behaviours irritate us, get under our skin, or drive us crazy – disobedience, whining, sibling rivalry, moodiness, cheekiness, not putting things away, not completing chores, laziness, not doing homework, lying . . . without warning, you are ready to blow your top.

Make a list of specific behaviours that trigger your emotions. Was it what was said? Tone of voice? A certain behaviour? The time of day? The more specific you are, the more likely you can stay calm when facing similar situations in the future.

2. RECOGNISE WARNING SIGNS.

Emotional 'red flags' signal that we are about to get angry: for example, a racing heart, a red or flushed face, balled fists, clenched teeth, tight muscles, yelling and shouting. Take note of how your body reacts just prior to full-blown anger. Before you can change how you react to your child, you must recognise warning signs that signal: 'Anger is on its way.'

3. A PLAN OF ACTION.

Let's say you have a nightly bedtime issue with Tyrone. He argues and dilly-dallies, and you end up yelling and losing it. (The trigger is bedtime.)

Next, note what you feel first – heart pounding (your warning sign). Now implement your plan of action. Take a few deep breaths, letting them out slowly, or perhaps an adult time-out. Now you are prepared to correct the situation without anger.

Here are some plans that have worked for other parents:

- Adult time out – go to another room or for a walk
- Deep breathing – letting breaths out slowly
- Prayer
- Daily workouts at a gym
- Wearing a rubber band on the wrist and snapping it when anger rises
- Calling a friend and discussing the situation
- Counting to 10 – slowly!

Learning to stay calm won't happen overnight: but don't give up. Certain situations require that you raise your voice to correct a behaviour; but, instead of getting angry, a firm, no-nonsense approach can correct the problem and model for your child a positive way of handling problems. Controlling your anger prepares you to put the other strategies into practice.

Strategy 2: Gain and maintain respect

The respect that a child maintains for his parents is in direct proportion to the respect he'll hold for the police force, teachers, school authorities, the Church, laws of the land and society in general. Where is respect learned? At the feet of Mum and Dad from the time he is born. When he is treated and spoken to with respect, he learns he is worthy of respect and how to respect others. When he sees Mum and Dad treat each other with respect, he learns about respect. Respect for self and others cannot be absorbed in an atmosphere of anger, however.

Respect is very much a two-way street. Mum should not expect respect from Jason if she doesn't treat him with respect. Mum should not embarrass or belittle him in front of his friends. Dad should not be critical of or sarcastic to Randall if he expects respect back. Randall may fear Dad enough that he dare not allow feelings of hate and revenge to surface at that moment, but they will emerge in future years.

Parents who gain and maintain their child's respect during the early years will have his respect during the teen years. And parents must realise that if they aren't worthy of respect, neither is their religion, their morals, their country or any of their standards. Children are keen observers and exceptionally perceptive.

PARENTING: THE BEST THAT YOU CAN BE

Never expect your children to grant you more respect than they see you give to your own parents.

Respect vanishes when anger appears. When anger surfaces, fear and rebellion take over in a child. The most important lessons learned in life are not reading, writing and arithmetic, as some suppose, but respect, obedience, reverence and self-control. These must be taught patiently, tenderly, lovingly and consistently, every day, so as to become a part of the child's character development.

Strategy 3: Set limits

My hometown of Tacoma, Washington, is famous for its ill-fated Narrows Bridge, which collapsed due to wind-induced vibrations after being open to traffic for only four months. The bridge stretched like a steel ribbon linking Tacoma with the Olympic Peninsula. The bridge quickly earned the nickname 'Galloping Gertie' from its rolling, undulating behaviour. Motorists felt as though they were riding a roller coaster while watching cars ahead completely disappear, as if dropping into a huge rolling wave.

The following account graphically describes what happened the day the bridge went down. 'Just as I drove past the towers, the bridge began to sway violently from side to side. Before I realised it, the tilt became so violent that I lost control of the car. . . . I jammed on the brakes and got out, only to be thrown onto my face against the kerb. . . . Around me I could hear concrete cracking. I started to get my dog Tubby, but was thrown again before I could get to the car. The car itself began to slide from side to side on the roadway. On hands and knees most of the time, I crawled 500 yards or more to the towers. . . . My breath was coming in gasps; my hands and knees were raw and bleeding from gripping the concrete kerb. . . . At the toll plaza I saw the bridge in its final collapse and saw my car plunge into the Narrows.'[1]

In your imagination allow me to take you as a tourist to visit my hometown. One of the scenic spots we'll visit is the new Tacoma Narrows Bridge. As we approach the 'on' ramp, we note that the bridge is intact, except for one thing: the guardrails at the sides of the bridge have been removed! How do you feel about crossing the bridge with me now? Fearful? I promise you I have no intention of driving over the edge – with or without guardrail – into one of the world's choppiest and most treacherous channels. The lesson is evident – we feel more secure when the guardrails are in place.

The analogy to children and setting limits is simple: there is security within defined limits. A happy home always involves limits.

> **Setting limits is one of the most important skills of parenting. Limits keep children safe and healthy. Limits also socialise them enough so they can function happily both inside and outside the home.**

And, if we do it right, our children will internalise the ability to set limits for themselves – the ultimate goal in discipline. Learning to live by limits is an important part of emotional growth and maturity. Only by learning to live within limits do we learn what is appropriate and acceptable.

Children begin testing limits while babies. Should a toddler throw food on the floor, he needs to learn that food belongs on his plate, not on the floor. If a warning fails, put him in his playpen and let him wail. Isolation is the consequence here. If a youngster bites or hits his brother, let him know this is not acceptable behaviour. The consequence here

Chapter 3 // Obedience: Developing your strategies

might be to sit him in a corner or send him to his room – isolate him.

Children continue testing limits throughout childhood. It reaches an all-time high during adolescence as the teenager requests privileges and more independence. By testing limits, the child learns about rules in the home and beyond. Your child needs to know what you will permit and what you will prohibit. Specific limits ought to be as few as possible, but reasonable and enforceable. Limits also need to be withdrawn or modified as a child grows older. When a child is aware of the limits, he doesn't get into trouble unless he deliberately asks for it. As long as he determines to stay within the limits, there is security and peace.

However, when a child continually tests the limits, it can cause problems for the whole family. Let's look in on Johnny, who has just been caught stealing a bar of chocolate. (Johnny has probably stolen before – this is just the first time he's been caught.) The store manager calls his parents. His parents punish him. No TV for a week. Three days into the punishment, Mum comes home from work and catches him watching TV. Poor Mum. She doesn't know what to do. She's never been much of a disciplinarian and certainly doesn't know how to set limits. Johnny has also learned that Mum can't follow through. Mum loses control while Johnny gains control. Johnny has learned he can steal and get away with it.

Johnny steals again. Mum sets up another limit. No talking on the phone for one week. But there is no one at home to monitor this limitation. Mum comes home and finds him on the phone. She dishes out another unenforceable punishment and weak warnings and forgets about it. Johnny finds a way around all limits set for him. He's had a lot of practice. He's been doing it since he was 2. One by one, every limit is tested and decimated. Now Johnny is in control. Mum can't control him, and neither can his teacher, nor the principal. Johnny's going to have trouble when he goes away to camp and every other place. Everyone has trouble with Johnny because Johnny figures he can

51

PARENTING: THE BEST THAT YOU CAN BE

do anything he wants. He never learned to accept limits on his behaviour.

> **What if you have a Johnny at home?**
>
> If you are a parent with a Johnny, you can still do something about this. But you had better work fast because the older Johnny gets, the more trouble you'll have. First, toughen up. If you catch Johnny lying, stealing, cheating, swearing or whatever, give appropriate discipline immediately. Don't hang back hoping he'll change. Dish out consequences for misbehaviour. Be firm, reasonable and loving. Then follow through. If you can't be present to monitor a punishment that needs monitoring, select another punishment!

One more step: call Johnny's bluff. He's already learned he can get his own way and that no one can control him. He may begin to make threats: 'If you don't let me do so and so, I'll run away from home. . . . I'll quit school. . . . I won't go to church anymore. . . .' Parents lose it when their kids say this. Do not be intimidated by such threats. Most kids don't want to lose the privileges they already have. Don't back down from the limits you have set.

Through the process, keep your cool. Don't blow it now by overreacting. Keep your temper in check. Johnny needs the reassurance and security that come from a controlled response. Set appropriate boundaries, and then follow through with consequences as necessary rather than reacting with rage.

Some parents – particularly permissive parents – hate setting limits. They are afraid their child will throw a tantrum or become angry with them. In the end, they find their child cannot manage his behaviour and is referred to by others as 'spoiled' because he appears to get his own way.

Other parents boast that their kids jump with quick obedience the minute they are spoken to. Children raised under this type of authoritarian rule often don't have good judgement or the ability to think for themselves. Later on such children will be more apt to follow the crowd, become bullies or victims, have difficulty managing their anger, and, as adults, be more prone to depression.

Children need limits, but, in the end, it is how you set them that counts. Setting limits means you have the courage to say 'No' and the ability to enforce them. But it also involves how those limits are set. While tongue lashings, deprecating remarks and harsh physical treatment harm a child's view of himself, setting reasonable limits appropriate for a child's age and ability actually builds self-worth. When a child knows how to manage himself in a variety of environments, he feels competent and qualified to move successfully through his day.

Strategy 4: Teach with clear and positive expectations

The long-range goal in discipline is to teach a child to guide his own behaviour, to make good decisions, to reason clearly about choices, to solve problems on his own and to plan ahead. When a child understands what behaviour is expected and the consequences of his behaviour, he can make better decisions even when parents are not there. A child who has been taught to reason

Chapter 3 // Obedience: Developing your strategies

will make better decisions and be more responsible. Clear expectations should be in place before a child does something he isn't supposed to do.

Disciplining with clear expectations can head off many problem behaviours. Always check to make certain your expectations are appropriate for the child's age and ability, remembering there are limits to what can be expected from children of all ages.

Here's how to teach a child through clear expectations:

1. CLEARLY EXPLAIN WHAT YOU REQUIRE IN ADVANCE OF MISBEHAVIOUR.

'You may go outside to play when your chores are done – bed made, room straightened and clothes hung up.' 'I need you home immediately after school today or by 3.30pm because we have to leave for Rachel's meeting at church.' 'After all your homework is complete and I have checked it, you may play video games on the computer.' 'Drive slowly through the construction area by Grandma's house, as fines are doubled in such zones.'

2. SPECIFY EXACTLY WHAT BEHAVIOURS YOU REQUIRE.

'Clean your room!' isn't specific enough. Nor is 'Come home after school,' or 'Get your homework done,' or 'Don't you dare speed today!' Such fuzzy requests leave too many loopholes for sloppy or half-completed chores and misunderstandings. They also leave the door wide open for arguments.

When the expectation is specific and clear, the child cannot make excuses for doing half the job.

3. STATE YOUR EXPECTATIONS IN A POSITIVE MANNER.

Expectations are clearer and more effective when they are positive rather than negative. In other words, teach a child what he should do rather than what not to do. Rather than saying, 'Stop rolling your eyes when I ask you to do something,' say instead, 'When you are asked to do something around the house, I'd appreciate it if you'd say, "OK, Mum, I'd be happy to help."' 'As soon as you get home today I want you to start your homework,' not: 'Don't you dare sneak off after school to play video games!' 'I want you to enjoy our new living room furniture as much as I do by taking care of it. Please remove your shoes before climbing on it, and eat only at the kitchen table.' Not: 'Get your dirty shoes off my couch!' 'Remember to slow down through construction zones,' rather than: 'Don't you dare speed through construction zones!'

PARENTING: THE BEST THAT YOU CAN BE

4. CHECK TO SEE IF THE CHILD UNDERSTANDS WHAT THE EXPECTED BEHAVIOUR IS.

Have your child repeat back what the expected behaviour is. This clarifies that he heard what was said and understands it. Then, if he chooses not to comply with your clear message, punishment will be easier to handle since the child ignored what was understood. He can't say, 'I didn't know,' or, 'I didn't hear you say that.'

5. SAY IT BACK ONE MORE TIME.

When the child responds, say the whole thing back one more time. 'That's right. You may go outside to play just as soon as your chores are done, bed made, room straightened and clothes hung up.' 'Yes, you must be home by 3.30 as I have to get Rachel to the church by 4 for her meeting.' 'Right, after your homework is done and I have checked it, you can play video games on the computer.' 'Yes, drive slowly through the construction zone.' This type of training definitely takes more time, but clarifies what is expected in everyone's mind.

6. ASK THE CHILD TO GIVE YOU A REASON FOR THE EXPECTED BEHAVIOUR.

'Tell me why it is a better choice to get your chores done before going out to play.' 'Why is it smarter for you to get home on time today?' 'Please explain why I'm asking you to get your homework done and checked prior to getting on the computer?' 'Sandra, tell me why I am asking you to slow down through the construction zone.'

When you take the time to help a child understand the reasons behind what has been asked for, he will more readily accept and learn from it.

7. APPLY CONSEQUENCES SHOULD THE CHILD FAIL TO COMPLY.

'Since you didn't get your chores done, there will be no TV tonight.' 'Since you made Rachel late for her meeting, you will have to miss football practice this week.' 'Since you've not been getting your homework done, there will be no computer games until you get caught up.' 'You know my rule about safe driving, so there will be no driving for one week. And you have to earn the money to pay for your ticket.'

Selecting appropriate consequences when a child fails to obey is another major parental art. In the above situations, the parent used deprivation of the car, TV or computer, and 'grounding' or missing football practice. 'Time out', or sending a child to his room, is especially effective for younger children as a consequence. But as a child gets older, his room is often where he prefers to be – with the privacy of his phone, stereo system, computer and TV. Make certain when restricting the privileges of an older child that you don't take everything away at once, or it will leave you with little or no leverage.

Parents cannot apply consequences appropriately when angry. They cannot conceal their anger from the child. Their tone of voice and facial expressions will give them away. Try to view the situation as if the child were a neighbour's child, not your own.

> **Administer any consequences in a firm but friendly manner.**

Clear expectations make day-to-day living easier. They provide guidelines for parents in consistently training their child. By obeying these clear and reasonable expectations, a child learns to trust his parents. It trains him to look for reasons, perceive his own behaviour and make wise choices.

A home with the best discipline and the fewest disciplinary problems will be one where there are clear expectations. A child should be allowed to grapple with making choices under these expectations. Give guidance as needed, but allow a child to make as many choices as possible along the way. Some of his best life lessons will be learned by making wrong choices. When he makes wrong choices, punish appropriately and consistently. It's better that he learn his lessons about making wrong choices now than when he is 17.

PARENTING: THE BEST THAT YOU CAN BE

Strategy 5: Speak once, then act

Many parents find themselves screaming and threatening in order to get a child to obey. A better solution involves speaking once in a firm manner. If the child chooses not to obey within a reasonable timeframe, you should act, rather than scream.

Let's use this principle to get Harry to bed. Every night Harry resists while Mum insists. Empty threats, warnings and escalating anger follow. Mum is dead tired after hassling three kids all day, getting supper on the table and cleaning up. Now it's Harry's bedtime. But Harry doesn't feel like going to bed and begins hassling his already-harassed Mum. Through experience he knows exactly how to stall the procedure another thirty minutes. Mum begins by asking that he put his toys away and get into the bathtub. Harry knows this first request means little or nothing, and continues to play. Ten minutes later Mum recalls where she is in the bedtime battle and issues a more threatening warning. 'Harry Arthur Monroe, didn't you hear what I asked you to do?' Harry knows that when his Mum uses all three names the situation is more serious, but continues to ignore her. Ten more minutes pass before Mum notices that he still hasn't moved. Now Mum loses it: 'Harry, get in that tub right now! How many times do I have to tell you the same thing? You wear me out! If you don't get to bed right now, I'll . . .' Harry recognises this as more serious and begins to put his toys away, but watches to see if Mum's attention wanders once more.

Mum can never get immediate obedience from Harry. Harry only pays attention after multiple warnings and exaggerated threats. Even then he only moves when Mum comes at him with anger in her voice and an upraised arm. Poor discipline! Harry needs to learn to move the first time Mum speaks. If he doesn't the action is swift and immediate. 'Harry, for every minute after 8pm it takes you to get to bed, you will lose computer time [or TV time] or go to bed early tomorrow night.' Speaking once, and following through with appropriate consequences that deprive the child of a cherished privilege, will generally solve the problem.

Or Mum could use a timer – a purchased one, or one on the oven. She would require Harry to set the timer at 8pm for thirty more minutes of play. When the timer rings Harry would immediately put his toys away and turn off the timer. Having to get up and turn off the timer gets him headed towards the bathroom and puts more of the responsibility on him for obeying.

56

Strategy 6: Natural consequences

Letting children experience the consequences of their decisions is a 'hassle-free' method of discipline. Children learn from experience, just as adults do. We call it 'learning the hard way'. It works like this:

Kayla left her dirty clothes on the floor, 'forgetting' to put them in the hamper as she had been told. Nagging, scolding, and threatening did no good. Mum decided to teach her to put her clothes in the hamper through natural consequences. Mum explained in a firm but friendly voice that from now on she would only wash clothes that were placed in the hamper. A week later Kayla had only wrinkled, dirty clothes from the floor to wear and was very unhappy. This prompted Kayla to get her dirty clothing into the hamper as instructed.

In this case Mum put the responsibility for getting clothes into the hamper on Kayla's shoulders, where it belongs. If Mum had picked up the clothes and washed Kayla's clothes anyway, she would have deprived her of learning responsibility for caring for her clothing.

> **Some parents would be embarrassed to have their child go to school in dirty, wrinkled clothing. But when parents protect a child from the consequences of her behaviour, the child lacks motivation to change that behaviour.**

Eleven-year-old Taylor left his baseball glove at the ball field and, when he went back for it, it was gone. He begged Dad for a new one. Dad wasn't very happy, since this was the third glove Taylor had lost this season. Dad scolded him and gave him a lecture on money, and about taking care of belongings and being responsible. But in the end Dad relented. 'All right. I'll get you one tomorrow, but this is the last one this summer! Promise me you won't lose this one.' (Dad had said the same thing when Taylor lost the second glove.)

Dad lost a golden opportunity to let natural consequences teach Taylor a valuable lesson. Because he felt sorry for Taylor, who couldn't play ball without a glove, he protected him from the consequences of his actions. Dad should have told Taylor that he could buy a new glove with his allowance. When Taylor bawled that he didn't have enough money to buy one, Dad should have told him kindly but firmly that he would have to wait until he did.

Natural consequences can be used in numerous ways. When a child doesn't do her homework, she will get a low grade. If she dawdles, she will be late. If she fails to get chores done, she may have to work through supper. If she doesn't come home on time for a meal, she'll go hungry. Hunger is the natural consequence of not eating. Later, when the child begs for something to eat, Mum explains that she is sorry that she is hungry and assures the child she'll have a hearty breakfast ready in the morning. The child who experiences the unpleasant consequences of her choices will be less likely to act like that again.

PARENTING: THE BEST THAT YOU CAN BE

Parents should explain beforehand what the consequences are for breaking a house rule. If the child knows the consequence of coming late for dinner is to miss a meal, then she has a choice. She can come on time to eat, or be late and go hungry. She has a choice, and the sooner she learns the consequences of her choices, the easier life will get for all involved. The child also needs to know the reason for the consequence: for example, it is extra work to have to feed her at another time and inconsiderate to the family.

When natural consequences are pleasant, the child will continue with the same behaviour. When natural consequences are unpleasant, the child will be motivated to change. Using natural consequences can help a child develop a sense of responsibility. It leads to warmer relationships between parent and child and to fewer conflicts. Allowing natural consequences to take over provides powerful opportunities for the child to make right choices.

> **One caution: Parents cannot use natural consequences if the health or safety of the child is involved.**
>
> If a child runs into the street without looking, you cannot wait till he is hit by a car to teach him the consequences of running into the street. If you do, you could end up with an injured child. Instead the child should be taken into the house and told firmly, 'Since you ran into the street, you cannot play outside now. You can go out again when you decide to stay out of the street.' This is a logical consequence. Again he has a choice. He can stay out of the street, or he can stay inside and play.

Managing the strong-willed child

Some children are extremely strong-willed. In spite of discipline, the strong-willed child will continuously repeat a misbehaviour. Why? To gain control over the parent. Even though he is punished time and time again for the same misbehaviour, punishment does not deter him from defying his parent. This child is engaged in a power struggle with his parent. Thus, the parent needs to be geared up for a long and strenuous battle. The parent must become stronger, more consistent and more patient – determined to outlast the child's stubborn behaviour.

Parents with a difficult or strong-willed child should not be blamed because their child refuses to sleep through the night, screams when left with a sitter or acts up in public. Frequently parents of more compliant children fail to understand how difficult it is to deal with such a child. As parents of a Marvellous Margareta who sleeps through the night, rarely fusses, smiles, coos and giggles most of the time and never vomits, they think that if you would only use certain behavioural techniques your strong-willed child wouldn't act that way. Parents on both sides of the fence must understand that a strong-willed child will be difficult to handle, regardless of what disciplinary methods are used.

If you are struggling with a strong-willed child, how can you cope? First, recognise that your child is not deliberately trying to destroy your life. Second, recognise that you are not the cause of your child's difficulties. Third, stop comparing your child with an easy-to-raise child. Make any necessary changes in the child's life as painlessly

Chapter 3 // Obedience: Developing your strategies

and gradually as possible. This child will frequently need more love and attention than other children. See that he gets it. Respond to him in much the same way as you would to a strong-willed or difficult adult. Stay calm when he is irritable and enjoy him during his good spells.

When you are a full-time parent to a strong-willed and difficult child, cut back on your hours if you have a demanding job. Leave him with grandma or a babysitter at least once a week while you take a turn at something creative and nurture other positive relationships in your life.

Even though this child will challenge your patience, tax your ability and test your creativity, do not give up on him or her! Do not blame yourself for the child's problems. Make sure you improve your resources on how to cope with a strong-willed child. Then lean on a higher Power for strength and courage to meet the next problem right around the corner.

It is a difficult experience to battle the strong-willed child, but tremendous rewards will be reaped in all the years to come from efforts expended today.

PARENTING: THE BEST THAT YOU CAN BE

Don't punish yourself

Often the punishments you impose on a child can inconvenience you as much as they do your child. There's no way of avoiding that. You must make some sacrifices in order to correct and guide a child properly. But don't let this go too far. If need be you can skip a golf date in order to show a teen you mean business. But you don't have to cancel a long-planned vacation. Simply postpone the punishment until your return. Mark your calendar or you are sure to forget!

Taming the arguer

The incessant arguer often thinks of himself as a debater. This idea is reinforced by those who tell him that he'll make a great lawyer someday. Presto! Therefore the first rule in taming the arguer is to refrain from referencing creative arguing skills. Talking about them only makes the arguer more determined to argue until he wins.

Sometimes a child's arguing skills are so exasperating that you say 'No' before you've heard the request. But a 'No' only brings out the best in a creative arguer! Let's look in on Jacob, who has just heard 'No' to his request. Now Jacob follows you from room to room trying to convince you of the brilliance of his argument until, out of frustration,

Chapter 3 // Obedience: Developing your strategies

desperation or guilt, you give in at least 50% of the time. Over time Jacob learns that, through persistent arguing, he can get you to change your mind if he perseveres. Half the time he can win. With a little luck he might be able to persuade Dad or Grandma to side with him against you. You feel trapped.

> **While it's important to encourage a child's critical thinking skills, arguing is a power struggle – not a discussion.**

The child gains valuable experience in manipulating and controlling the parent. This habit will make it difficult for him to live and work with others, including his parents.

Here's a plan for taming the arguer. Arguers are adept at engaging you at inconvenient times. They instinctively understand you are too busy to deal with the issue. When the request is made, rather than responding with a 'Yes' or 'No', ask the reason for the request. Hear him out and then say, 'Let me think about it and I'll get back to you in a few minutes.' (For a big request, longer.) This gives you time for rational thinking and teaches the child patience. Since you have not yet responded, you'll probably get some good behaviour during the waiting period.

PARENTING: THE BEST THAT YOU CAN BE

Think through his request and the reasons for it. Seek advice from your husband or wife when necessary and possible. If you give the thumbs-up to his request, smile; be positive and enthusiastic. If your response is 'No', say so firmly while backing up your refusal with a reason. Once the final word has been delivered, absolutely never, ever change your decision. Engage in no further dialogue concerning the matter, regardless of his behaviour. Don't allow him to make you feel guilty. The sooner he learns he cannot have everything he asks for, the better off you'll both be.

Should he begin to argue his point again, calmly state that you've heard his arguments and assessed them, and the discussion is over. Don't get duped into another discussion. Should he continue to argue, time out may become necessary. The arguer must learn that the parent has the right to say 'No'. Consistency in dealing with the arguer will soon provide you with a more pleasant and positive home and a child who respects you.

The last word

Family specialists agree that using threats and put-downs interferes with a child's healthy development. They also agree that the perfect formula that fits every disciplinary situation does not exist. All children are unique, and so is every family in which they live. A strategy that works for one parent might not work for another.

Effective discipline does, however, preserve the child's self-worth and dignity. Actions that insult or belittle the child can inhibit learning and teach the child to be unkind to others. Actions that affirm the child's efforts and progress, no matter how slow or small, are likely to encourage healthy development.

Teaching a child to obey so he can become self-disciplined is a demanding task. It demands patience, thoughtful attention and a good understanding of your child. However, helping your child achieve self-discipline is worth the effort. It is foundational for his lifelong personal and character goals.

Footnote

[1] *http://en.wikipedia.org/wiki/Tacoma_Narrows?Bridge_(1940)*

CHAPTER 4

What counts is character

> 'The best way to teach character is to have it around the house.'
> Unknown

Rosalie Elliot, an 11-year-old from South Carolina, was in the fourth round of a national spelling contest. Her voice trembled as she softly spelled out the word 'avowal' in her Southern accent. Due to her accent and the softness of her voice, the judges had difficulty determining if she had said 'a' or 'e' for the next-to-the-last letter.

The proceedings had been recorded but even after several replays the judges still could not determine what she had said. Only one person really knew what Rosalie had said – Rosalie. The judges finally asked her. By now Rosalie had already heard the correct spelling whispered repeatedly by the audience. But when asked, without hesitation, she replied, 'I misspelled the word,' and walked off the stage. The audience responded with a standing ovation for Rosalie's honesty and integrity.[1]

Rosalie Elliot was already displaying incredible character traits at the age of 11. Where were these traits learned? At home: at the feet of Mum and Dad, as they conducted their lives with integrity.

What does it mean to have 'character'? We know what it means when we say someone has 'personality'. Someone with personality has charm, winning ways and a pleasantness that makes him likeable.

Character goes beyond the externals of personality and has more to do with the inner qualities not visible to the naked eye: qualities like moral excellence and integrity. It involves honesty, self-control, thoughtfulness to others, religious loyalty, moral ideals, conscience and the ability to inhibit impulses.

Character goes beyond just doing the right things. It takes in pure thoughts and feelings, and includes pure motives. Out of such fine inner qualities one will then be able to make right choices and have pure speech, behaviour and habits.

The long-range goal of raising a child with character is to help him develop such habits to the point that, even when you are not present, he would still make right choices.

PARENTING: THE BEST THAT YOU CAN BE

Teaching a child to make good decisions

How can parents prepare their child to make good decisions? An endless variety of situations demanding a decision surface daily – how to spend birthday money from Grandma, choice of friends, whether to cheat on a test, take drugs, go to Sue's house when her parents aren't there, or come home on time. As your child gets older, the situations increase in risk, frequency and danger. And most of the time you aren't going to be there. The best teaching opportunities, then, occur when the child is young. This prepares him to make more difficult choices later on.

Here are five easy-to-use steps that can be adapted to most situations. They allow the parent to help a child to think more clearly, develop sound reasoning abilities and eventually make worthwhile decisions.

1. IDENTIFY THE PROBLEM/ISSUE.

A child isn't always aware there is a problem. A 13-year-old may not think that skipping breakfast is a problem. He only wants more sleep. An 8-year-old may not think spending hours playing computer games harmful. He only thinks of having fun now.

When teaching a child to identify the issue, ask specific, open-ended questions like, 'After you were invited to do that, what happened next?' Who, what, where, why and how questions will help you help your child get a clear picture of the situation. Avoid questions that can be answered with one-word responses like 'Yes' or 'No'. Once you identify the problem, briefly rephrase what happened and send it back for verification, asking if that description is accurate.

2. BRAINSTORM POSSIBLE SOLUTIONS TO THE PROBLEM.

Since a child has limited reasoning ability till age 10 or so, he will often have a limited perception of what his options are. Questions like, 'What other choices were open to you at that time?' or, 'If you had another chance to respond, what would you say?' may not be meaningful to him.

You may want to take over and tell your child what he should have done. But that tactic doesn't help a child learn to make decisions. Guide your child into thinking through at least three options, making sure that one is reasonable. More than three gets confusing! If your child has trouble coming up with one, you may suggest something, but only after allowing the child to think it through first.

3. LIST THE PROS AND CONS FOR EACH SOLUTION.

Ask your child what his thoughts are about each suggestion: 'What's good about this idea? Do you see any disadvantages?' This step may require some input from you, especially for the young child, or during the early stages of initiating the decision-making process. Since most of us are very visual, a written list of the advantages and disadvantages would assist in providing a clear picture of the best option. It would also help your child to see the connection between the option and the consequences or end result of making that choice.

4. SELECT THE BEST SOLUTION.

Briefly summarise the pros and cons and ask your child to choose the one he thinks will work best. Make sure he understands the consequences that may result from each option listed. Some decisions are more difficult to make, and it might be wise to give time for additional thought and processing and come back to re-evaluate the situation again at a later time if it isn't urgent.

5. ALLOW THE CHILD TO SUFFER THE CONSEQUENCES OF HIS DECISION.

A child needs to live with the consequences of his decision. To teach this as well as the value of money to their five children, one doctor gave each child a specified sum of money to purchase his own clothing at the beginning of the school year. One boy overspent on expensive shoes and a 'really cool' jacket. Later that year he spilled paint on his favourite jeans. Holes might be 'cool' but paint was not, so he begged Dad for a new pair so he wouldn't be considered a jerk. Even though Dad could have provided him with another pair of jeans, this boy had to wear his paint-splashed jeans until his next clothing allowance. The temporary humiliation taught this young man a much more valuable lesson than giving in and rescuing him. He learned to make better decisions about how much to spend and how much to save for emergencies.

Encourage your child to make as many decisions on his own as he can, but always emphasise that you are there for input if needed. Later check on how things went. If things went well, pass on the praise. When a bad choice has been made, empathise as he suffers the consequences. But do not play 'Rescuer' or your child will never learn to make good decisions.

Beginning with small problems first gives your child time to get comfortable with the process of decision-making. This practical approach to making decisions can be applied to multiple situations. Once you start using

PARENTING: THE BEST THAT YOU CAN BE

this method you can be confident that you have given your child a head-start in making better decisions that will benefit him his entire life.

Building better habits

'My son is so selfish! How can I teach him to share?' 'My daughter is mean to her friends. What can I do to teach her to treat others with respect and kindness?' 'How can I help my child not to lie?' 'John is totally irresponsible and never remembers to do anything. How can I help him to change?'

Isolated incidents do not ruin character. They may concern you, but it is the repetition of any behaviour that forms a habit. And habits form character. Therefore, every time a child misbehaves and gets away with it, a pattern is developing that distorts character development.

> **Every time a child repeats a positive course of action, character is also being developed. Thoughts form actions. Actions form habits. Habits form character.**

How can parents help a child develop positive habits? The chapter on discipline dealt with the proper training and response for a child's defiant behaviour. But there are countless situations that do not involve a direct challenge to authority that can be used in helping a child develop better habits. How can a parent teach honesty, responsibility with chores, proper table manners, courtesy or kindness? How can a parent curb lying, whining, dawdling, sloppiness and negative traits of character?

Enter – 'the law of reinforcement'

The most effective technique for building better habits involves the law of reinforcement. This law states: 'Behaviour that achieves desired consequences will recur.' Simply stated, if a child likes what happens as a result of his behaviour, he will do it again. If he enjoys tormenting his mother by not going to bed when asked, he will continue to do it. However, when he is strongly rewarded for getting to bed on time through something he wants, he is more likely to get to bed on time.

> **Unfortunately, many mums and dads do not know how to use the law of reinforcement properly.**

Mum had a great deal of difficulty managing 4-year-old Patti. Patti had developed many bad habits and was often referred to as a little 'pig'. She would open the refrigerator door, remove various dishes of food, and consume as much as she could. Neither reasoning with her nor spankings had any effect on this behaviour.

A second set of inappropriate behaviours involved screaming. When Patti failed to get what she wanted, she let loose with a series of sharp, ear-splitting screams that brought nearby adults quickly to her rescue. If Patti and another child at the nursery school were playing with a toy that Patti wanted, she would try to take it away. If the other child resisted, Patti would scream loudly, and kept screaming until the other child dropped the toy or an adult came to give the toy to Patti to stop the piercing screams.

A third set of behaviours involved toilet training. Whenever Patti didn't want to do

Chapter 4 // What counts is character

something that someone was trying to force her to do, she said, 'Oh! Oh! B. M.' (meaning Bowel Movement). And she produced one on cue. By the time Patti and her clothes were cleaned up the argument was usually resolved in Patti's favour.

Patti was born with a marked amount of brain injury. To complicate matters, when she was eighteen months of age she became deathly ill and lost almost a quarter of her body weight. Because of her physical problems, her behaviours were never normal. She also had limited ability to communicate.

But it was Patti's behavioural problems that brought her to the attention of a therapist. After observing Patti for some time, he determined that she had learned many inappropriate ways of getting what she wanted. She couldn't tell people what she wanted to eat, so she grabbed whatever was handy. If she wanted something that was not easily given to her, she would scream until she got it. If someone threatened to punish her if she didn't stop doing what she wanted to do, she soiled her pants.

Careful observation showed that Patti's parents and nursery school teachers unwittingly rewarded Patti's bad behaviour by giving her what she wanted. Her parents insisted that they reprimanded and spanked her for getting into the refrigerator: but she got what she wanted anyway. The teachers also said they punished her: but the punishment was too mild, and she got so much attention for bad behaviour that it was reinforced rather than extinguished.

Upon learning Patti was fond of cookies, the therapist made clever use of these as rewards. The therapist would point to milk, and say, 'Patti, this is milk. Can you say "milk"?' Patti couldn't say 'milk', but if she uttered any sound at all the therapist gave her a small animal cookie. After a time Patti could utter a sound more like 'milk'. She began learning new words in minutes. Next the parents were instructed to make no fuss at all if they found her in the refrigerator. They were instructed quietly to take the food away and to lead her out of the kitchen and sit her on a stool for five minutes while saying nothing.

One day the therapist was working with Patti in an enclosed room when she played her trump card of soiling herself to get her way. For thirty minutes the therapist continued as if nothing had happened, even though the stench was nauseating. Once Patti learned she couldn't get her way by soiling herself or screaming, she shifted to a more mature and approved manner of getting what she wanted.

PARENTING: THE BEST THAT YOU CAN BE

Patti's objectionable behaviours dropped to nearly zero within a short period of time, and follow-up observations showed a continuing good interaction between Mum and Patti and an absence of objectionable behaviours. Patti was receiving more affection from her mother and was approaching her in more affectionate ways. Patti's mother learned that, by following Patti's good behaviours with rewards of some kind and by consistently punishing objectionable behaviour, she could change Patti's behaviour.

You, too, can change your child's behaviour in the same manner by learning what behaviour to reinforce and how to extinguish negative behaviours by ignoring them.

Reinforce good behaviour

Three types of reinforcers are especially important to parents – social, activity and token. **Social reinforcers** involve words of praise, affirmation, attention, smiling, touching and being near. Some parents use social reinforcers instinctively; others must learn how to use them. **Activity reinforcers** involve granting privileges like playing a game, reading aloud, running errands, watching TV, having a party, playing outdoors, time on the computer, making cookies, helping with dinner, telling a joke and going first. Activities are powerful motivating tools, yet we frequently do not recognise and appreciate their usefulness.

Such things as points, stars, stamps, charts and money are **token reinforcers**. Token reinforcers are accumulated and then exchanged for a long-range goal. How does it work? Let's say you have a 10-year-old who obeys slowly, is unco-operative in getting chores or homework done, won't go to bed on time and needs constant reminding to practise her clarinet. Her behaviour can be changed with a chart and token reinforcers. To instigate a chart, the following steps are necessary:

1. DRAW UP A LIST OF RESPONSIBILITIES OR HABITS THAT NEED REINFORCING.

Ten to twelve responsibilities are appropriate for most children; fewer for a small child and more for an older child. Include some items that the child already does well, in order to make it easy to earn points, as well as negative behaviours that need to be changed. The chart might include the following behaviours:

Emily's Chart

- I changed clothes after school and hung them up.
- I made my bed and straightened my room before leaving for school.
- I fed the dog before breakfast.
- I put my toys away before bedtime.
- I studied my Bible lesson.
- I was in bed by 8.30pm.
- I obeyed the first time I was spoken to.
- I cleared the supper table and put dishes in the dishwasher.
- I practised my clarinet without being reminded.
- I got up when the alarm went off.

2. SELECT A 'PAY-OFF'.

What is your child willing to work for? The end 'prize' is what determines the success or failure of the chart. It might be a great pair of shoes or jeans, a computer game or a week at summer camp. Consider taping a picture of the pay-off on the chart to help your child visualise the goal.

3. ALLOW THE CHILD TO MARK THE CHART.

This should be done each night at bedtime while behaviours are still fresh in both your minds. Weight the most difficult tasks with the most points. You might make a rule that if your child fails to mark the chart at the end of the day or misses three items in one day, no points are awarded. You can also deduct points for misbehaviour.

4. TOTAL THE POINTS WEEKLY.

At the end of each week total the points, stars or money so the child can check on her progress.

5. KEEP THE CHART IN FORCE FOR FOUR TO SIX WEEKS.

Why four to six weeks? The goal is to build good habits. According to the **Reader's Digest Great Encyclopaedic Dictionary**, habits are 'an act or practice so frequently repeated as to become relatively fixed in character and almost automatic in performance.' Experts have calculated that, regardless of a person's age or sex, it takes twenty-one to forty-five days to change a habit. In other words, the child must repeat the action for twenty-one to forty-five days before it becomes a permanently fixed habit.

Should you find that your child still has difficulty performing a task listed on the chart, increase the reinforcer – double the points, stars or money. This system works wonders when the immediate reinforcer and the long-range goal are used correctly and are strong enough. One mother told me that she had tried the chart system but that it had failed. She had used money as the reinforcer, and in her words, 'It just didn't work.' After some questioning, I learned that her son was an active member of 4-H,* through which he raised and sold cattle. By the time he turned 9 he already had several thousand dollars in a bank account. Money was the wrong reinforcer for this child! We discussed changing the reinforcer to something the child really wanted – a weekend camping trip with Dad. After this the system worked beautifully.

After using the chart for four to six weeks, set it aside. Later you can use it to produce excellent results again. Charts must be adapted to the age of the child, but they are effective for children as young as 3 right through the teen years. (Later on in this chapter there's help in developing a chart for teenagers.)

PARENTING: THE BEST THAT YOU CAN BE

Parents often report the week following the initiation of a chart to be the most peaceful week of their lives! Why? Because the responsibility for their child's behaviour is off their shoulders and on their child's shoulders, where it belongs! Yet there remains a host of parents who take the responsibility for getting their child's homework completed and handed in on time, for getting their child up in the morning so he won't be late to school, or for driving his forgotten lunch money to school so he won't miss lunch.

When and how can such parents begin to understand that responsible behaviour will never be developed in a child by protecting him from the consequences of his behaviour? A child is more motivated to change negative traits when allowed to feel the full weight of responsibility for his actions, along with the consequences. When he fails to pull his weight, Mum and Dad must refuse to rescue him. They must step back and allow natural consequences to take over if they ever want to see positive character traits developed. In addition to suffering natural consequences, the youngster needs powerful motivators to help him learn to do what is right and avoid wrong choices and irresponsibility. Try it. You'll like the results.

*4-H is an international network of youth organisations that assists youth to achieve their full potential in a variety of ways, including entrepreneurship.

Overworked mums

When a woman works outside the home and has a family she really has two jobs. This takes a toll on women, their marriages and their children. As a result many women become stressed out, cross, and irritable. They feed their families fast foods, are too exhausted to make love, get behind in housework, send their kids to day care (even when the kids are sick), neglect their husbands and children – and feel guilty.

One study noted that women get twenty to twenty-five minutes less sleep a night than their husbands, who get a full seven to eight hours. Mothers of children under 3 years of age do even worse. They get forty-five to fifty minutes less sleep every night. The lack of sleep and the resulting tiredness take their toll on women and their families. This study also found that husbands had fifteen more hours of free time a week than their wives. Over a year this amounts to a month of free time to do what they wish while their wives raise the children and clean the house.

Behind their breezy, successful facades many superwomen are actually stressed out and resentful, or headed in that direction.

One mum suffered from constant fatigue. She worked as a nurse practitioner in a busy office. Every day she returned home and cooked nutritious meals, cleaned the house, paid the bills, and did the laundry and shopping. She shuttled the kids to their music lessons and after-school activities, and was present in the cheering section during their games. In other words, she did it all. But one day, exhaustion took over. She totally collapsed and simply could not move.

After a doctor's visit and some much-needed rest, she recognised that changes had to be made in her family. She gathered her husband and children for an urgent meeting and presented a list of chores that had to be completed weekly. Each was instructed to choose how he wished to help.

She planned a week's menu and assigned grocery shopping, table setting, cleaning up and three meals a week. Bill paying was turned over to her husband. That was fifteen years ago. Although the original plan has been modified repeatedly, it works.

Husbands and children should assist with household tasks, especially when Mum works outside the home. Paul asks us to 'share each other's burdens' (Galatians 6:2, NLT). This includes how we live together at home. It means that husbands, wives and children must work together to maintain common living space.

Here are a few creative ideas that can be put to use quickly and easily:

1. INITIATE A FAMILY CLEAN-UP HOUR.

A good share of housework has nothing to do with cleaning. Instead, it deals with clutter – putting things away. This problem can be solved by calling the entire family together at least once a week for TUT (Tidy Up Time). During this hour everyone pitches in and puts belongings away and tidies up the house.

Three things make this work:
1 Everyone takes part (even Dad).
2 Everyone works in teams. No one tackles a mess alone, even though only one person may have made it. While a daughter straightens her room, Dad vacuums. While Mum sorts through the clutter on the worktop, a son mops the kitchen floor.
3 No one stops or plays until either the work is done or sixty minutes are up – whichever comes first. TUT takes a tremendous load off Mum's shoulders and can be done more than once a week.

2. THE FIVE-MINUTE PICK-UP PLAN.

All family members take five minutes to tidy up before leaving their rooms in the morning. Make it a rule: 'Before coming to breakfast, hang up your towel, put your brush away and make your bed.' Just five minutes. Be firm, consistent and reasonable. Stay with it.

No adult should perform maid service for another adult or for a child who is old enough to go to school. Insist that family members pick up after themselves. If they fail to co-operate or 'forget', start a 'buy-back' basket. You pick up the item, and they buy it back for 25 cents (or a dollar, if you get desperate).

PARENTING: THE BEST THAT YOU CAN BE

Keep the money and treat yourself. You earned it!

3. POST A LIST OF JOBS.

People who don't ask for help rarely get it, especially if that pattern has been learned through prior experience by living in a family where Mum does everything. Why should anyone put anything away or become responsible when Mum does it for them?

When Mum gets sick and tired of being everyone else's servant, she'll find that written messages work wonders. Post a list of jobs to be done in a message centre. This eliminates 'I didn't know,' 'I forgot,' and other excuses. Every once in a while, provide a surprise or a reward. This keeps everyone reading the list and makes doing chores worthwhile.

4. USE REWARDS WISELY.

Make helping with chores pay off. Offer rewards after specific tasks are completed: 'Just as soon as the Lego, toys and clothes are picked up, you can call John and go to the park to play ball.' 'As soon as you get the lawn mowed, you can play a computer game.' 'As soon as the garage is swept out, I have a special treat for you.' 'As you dust, lift up each object and dust thoroughly, because I've hidden some money under objects that's yours to keep for helping me on this busy day.'

5. MAKE IT FUN TO WORK TOGETHER.

Make chores pleasant and fun. When a parent criticises, nags and complains, the family develops negative attitudes towards chores and helping. Working together in the garden, for example, with each person doing a different task, provides great opportunities for togetherness, communication, teaching, sharing and playing. The same technique can be used when cleaning the garage or house. Find things to laugh about. Add a song, tell a story, listen to music, whistle. Afterwards, play a game together, have a water fight, or head for the park. Exercise a little creativity and the family will learn that work can be fun. **What's learned with pleasure is learned full measure.**

When good work habits and attitudes have been established, the household will run more smoothly with less-stressed adults and children. The children will become more capable, responsible and reliable – traits that go a long way in building character. When active minds and hands are not directed towards useful tasks, they will find mischief to get into which can permanently damage character development. Work is the best discipline a child can have.

The impact of TV and media violence

FACT: The average child will have watched 100,000 acts of violence, including 8,000 murders, by the time s/he finishes the sixth grade. When the media industry is attacked they counter with: 'There is no proof. Millions watch TV without becoming criminals. We only give the public what they want.'

We live in an age when both parents work and children have an enormous amount of unsupervised time. It becomes essential that smart parents learn the facts about the effect of violent TV, movies and video games on children.

Studies by George Gerbner at the University of Pennsylvania show that children's TV programming contains about twenty acts of violence an hour. In one study, about 100 pre-school children were observed both before and after watching television. Half the group watched programmes with violent and aggressive acts, while the others watched programming with no violence. Those who watched the violent programmes struck out at their playmates, argued, disobeyed authority and were less willing to wait for things than those who watched non-violent shows. [2]

Some of the most compelling studies have investigated children's behaviour before and after being introduced to television. University of British Columbia researchers compared the levels of aggression in Canadian 6-to-8-year-olds who had access to TV and another group who had no access due to a mountain range. When television was eventually available in the town without previous access, the hitting, biting and shoving levels of the children increased 160%! [3]

University of Michigan psychologist Leonard Eron launched a landmark longitudinal study on 800 8-year-olds. He found that children who watched more violent TV were more aggressive in the playground and in the classroom. These students were checked on eleven and twenty-two years later. These same aggressive children grew up to be more violent 19- and 30-year-olds who caused

PARENTING: THE BEST THAT YOU CAN BE

more domestic violence and got more traffic tickets. Even if they were not more aggressive as children, they were more aggressive as adults.[4]

Studies from 2005 show that the less television watched between the ages of 8 and 11, the greater the probability of success at school. The quality of what is watched on TV closely matches the child's level of success later on. Watching less TV increases the odds of a child finishing university. It was also noted that having a TV in the bedroom contributed to lower grades and/or failure.[5]

Hundreds of other studies show that children and teenagers may become immune or numb to the horror of violence, accept violence as the way to solve problems, imitate the violence they see on TV, or identify with characters (victims or victimisers).

Sometimes watching only one episode of violence increases aggressiveness. Children who watch more realistic violence and see it repeated frequently or go unpunished are more likely to act it out. Children with emotional, behavioural or learning problems are more easily influenced by TV violence. The impact of violence may be noted immediately or it may lay dormant until a later time.

Video games

Children are spending increasing amounts of time playing video and computer games – an average of thirteen hours a week for boys and five hours a week for girls. Because these games are a newer medium, there is less research on them than there is on TV and movies. But early findings indicate that such games have an even stronger effect on children's aggression, because they are more highly engaging and interactive; they reward violent behaviour, and these behaviours are repeated over and over, every time the game is played. Video and computer games are unlike going to a violent movie. Games use techniques already effective in teaching people to drive cars, fly planes, or go to war – simulation.

> **Simulation hones the trainee's instincts and helps him build habits that can be acted out quickly without a second thought.**

Games laced with human atrocities help young, impressionable minds practise killing without care. This teaches children that when they experience anxiety, rather than calming themselves or talking to someone about it, they can act out by kicking, hitting or even killing.

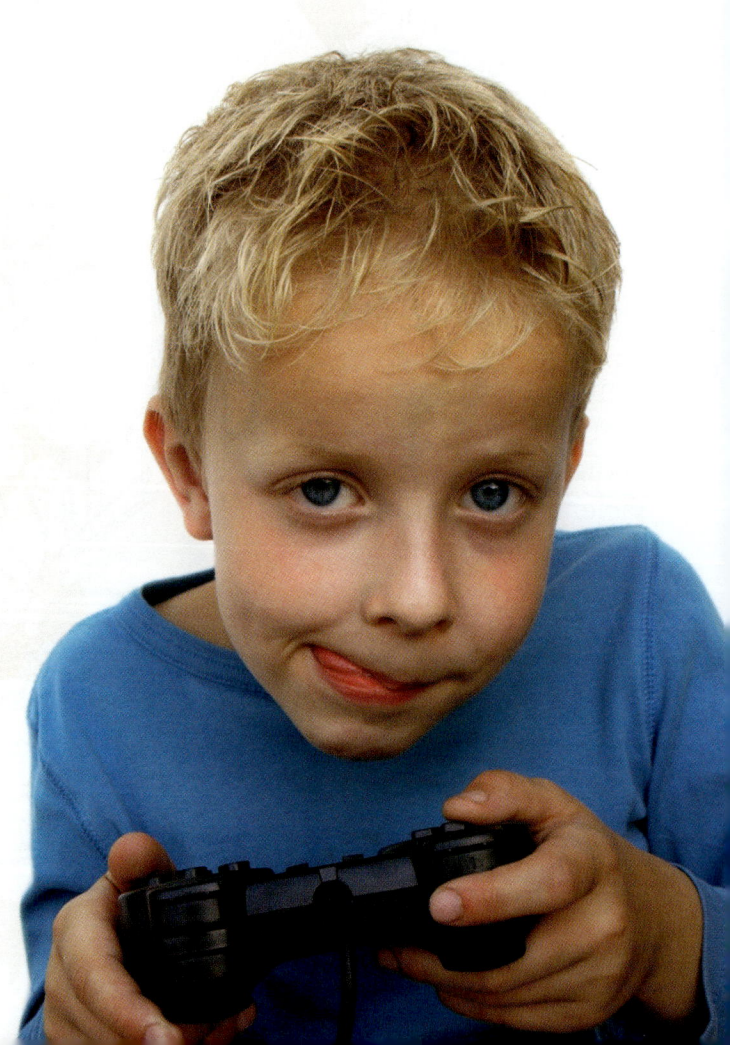

Chapter 4 // What counts is character

Some well-known video and computer games make victims into something less than human. The youngster holds the joystick or sits at the keyboard and holds guns and axes. Young players practise cutting heads off while watching blood spurt from the necks of victims. Over and over they rehearse shooting police officers. Dead bodies are kicked and urinated on. Every time a youngster plays a violent video game, he is in simulation. He practises humiliating others, laughs at their pain, says things to dehumanise his victim and justifies the murder.

> **Violent games imply that there are no consequences to breaking moral values. Instead of going to jail if you shoot someone, you get extra points!**

Occult themes are some of the most popular games and always include witchcraft and magic. Instead of God being victorious, the devil is portrayed as strong. Familiarity with the occult poses real dangers.

How can parents minimise the danger of such games to their child?

Here are some tips:

> **Set limits.**
> If you are worried over how much time your child spends playing games, limit the amount of time or specify a time when games can be played.

> **Put game space in a public area.**
> Just as with the internet, keep the game-playing area public so it is easier to monitor what games are being played.

PARENTING: THE BEST THAT YOU CAN BE

Play games with your child.
Know first-hand what your child is being exposed to and how he reacts to various features of the game.

Rent before you buy.
Many video stores rent games. Make a trial run before you buy.

Talk to other parents.
Get their reaction to certain games before you allow them in your house.

Familiarise yourself with game ratings.
Every video and computer game has a rating system for age appropriateness and content. But labels do not tell the whole story. Scenes that you may label as violent or sexual may not be seen in the same light by those who do the rating.

Helping teens respect boundaries

Boundaries are established limits – limits that are not to be crossed. Should a teen cross a boundary there must be consequences. When boundaries are maintained, a reward is appropriate. This way he learns that it pays to co-operate. When a parent establishes boundaries, the teen chooses whether to stay within the boundaries or go beyond. If he chooses to go beyond, he also chooses the consequences.

Parents who allow their teens to disregard boundaries and get away with wrong and irresponsible behaviour are training them to do wrong. For example, should parents allow their daughter to get away with disrespectful behaviour towards them, they are training her to be disrespectful towards other authority figures: and she is not learning self-control. This lack of adhering to boundaries now does not prepare her for the self-control she will need in adulthood. If parents allow their teen son repeatedly to come in after curfew, they are allowing him to disrespect time boundaries. Later in life he will have trouble holding a job because he never learned to respect time boundaries at home.

76

Chapter 4 // What counts is character

As a parent of a teenager, you have not only a right to set limits on choices your teen makes, but also a responsibility. Most teens want to be independent and do what they want to do. It may seem right to them but that doesn't make it right. This is why teens need their parents' guidance. And parents need to talk with their teens about limits and explain realistic consequences and rewards. Boundaries are designed to develop character. When a teen experiences consequences for defying a boundary, the painful consequences can be used to develop self-control.

Listed here are some boundary guidelines for activities most parents will face:

MUSIC.

According to some estimates, the average teenager listens to six hours of music a day – rock, rap, reggae, heavy metal or whatever is trending! It's their most devoted companion. To a large extent, it dictates what they wear, what they believe, and many of their other choices.

For years Christian leaders and parents have argued that rock music has a negative effect on our youth. But does it? David Merrell, a high school student in Suffolk, Virginia, won first prize in a state science fair to determine the effect of music on lab mice. He created a maze that took mice about ten minutes to negotiate. Then Merrell played classical music to one group and hard rock music to another group for ten hours a day. After three weeks the group exposed to classical music made it through the maze in about ninety seconds, while the group exposed to rock took thirty minutes! Merrell had to cut his experiment short, however, because the hard rock mice all killed one another! The mice listening to classical music did not do that.

One of the greatest causes of deafness in youth is the violent and harsh sounds of hard rock and heavy metal music. The damage to hearing is great, but the damage to the mind may be even greater.

Several troubling themes are prominent in some rock music: advocating and glamourising the use of drugs and alcohol; graphic violence; pictures and explicit lyrics presenting suicide as an alternative solution; preoccupation with the occult; songs about Satanism and human sacrifice, and the apparent enactment of these rituals during concerts; and sexual themes – sadism, masochism, incest, devaluing women and violence towards women. Studies on high school students show that nearly 75% of the girls who preferred heavy metal music had considered suicide, compared with 35% of the girls who preferred other types of music. [6]

A recent study by the American Medical Association on 279 popular songs showed

PARENTING: THE BEST THAT YOU CAN BE

that today's hit rock music contained a strong positive reference to drugs and alcohol. References to drugs were found in 41.6% of the songs. Rap music referred to substance abuse in a positive way 77% of the time, country music 36% of the time, and hip hop 20%.

Other reports alert us to the pulsating jungle beat and syncopated rhythms which cause a phenomenon known as nerve jamming, which is similar to hypnosis. A person listening to the beat of rock music literally loses conscious control of himself and is open to the message of drugs, immorality and violence through the musician. The listener is no longer in control of his body.

While hard rock and heavy metal music can harm the mind and soul, classical music has been shown to regenerate brain cells, and soothe and relax the body. It is often used in music therapy to aid in the healing process. Just as it helps plants to grow and mice to navigate mazes, the college entrance exam board reported that students with experience in musical performance scored 31 points higher on the verbal portion of their SAT and 39 points higher in the maths section than the national average. Preschoolers who studied piano scored 34% better in spatial and temporal reasoning ability than preschoolers who spent the same amount of time learning to use computers. [7]

Few people understand the powerful effect music has on the frontal lobe. Music enters the brain through the emotional regions, which include the temporal lobe and the limbic system. From there some kinds of music tend to produce a frontal lobe response that influences the will, moral worth and reasoning power. However, it appears it is not the harmonic or melodic structure of the music that's the culprit. It's the rhythms in rock music that tend to clash with or disrupt internal body rhythms. The disruption of these natural rhythms explains why rock music listeners are more prone to drug use and engaging in extramarital sex, and why heavy metal listeners are more likely to contemplate suicide. The disharmonic rock-like music also causes damage to the hippocampus and causes shrinking of the frontal lobe. [8]

On the other hand, harmonious music like hymns and symphonies can produce a positive frontal lobe response. Classical music has been demonstrated to help college students understand spatial relationships in geometry. And listening to Mozart piano sonatas significantly increases spatial-temporal reasoning. [9]

Obviously what a teen listens to will affect his behaviour, his hearing and his grades. You may be able to set limits on what your teen listens to at home, but not once he's out of the house. When a teenager is persistently preoccupied with music that has destructive themes, and there are changes in behaviour such as isolation, depression and alcohol or other drug abuse, an immediate psychological evaluation should be considered.

MOBILE PHONES.

Mobile phones have become a social necessity for teens, allowing them portable access to the social media and the opportunity to surf the internet at large. Teens agree mobile phones are more important than owning an iPod, computer, TV or gaming system. A mobile phone allows more than talking with friends – it enables texting. Texting is the teens' way of staying connected to their friends throughout the day and receiving quick responses. They do it late at night after parents are asleep. They do it in the classroom with their hands behind their backs. They do it so much their thumbs hurt!

Now teens have taken up 'sexting' – where users send sexually explicit images via their phones. Without realising the long-term consequences, they share these photos of themselves and others: and the results can be devastating.

Surveys estimate that about one third of all teens have mobile phones. Teens love them. Mum and Dad find them both a blessing and a curse. They are a blessing in helping parents stay in touch with their kids and for use in case of an emergency, but a curse in attempting to control hours spent on the phone, charges for excess minutes, text messaging and data. It gets even more complicated when teens buy their own phones and pay the bills, or if Grandma and Grandpa give them a phone. Can a parent monitor its use under such circumstances?

You can expect hassles over phone privileges. Therefore you might want to consider a contract to control mobile phone use. Contract or not, ground rules need to be set. These rules might include such things as: no mobile phone use or texting during class hours, no phoning or texting while driving, guidelines for phone use after school, no calls or texting during supper, no phoning or texting after 10pm.

When rules for the phone are abused there must be consequences. You may feel like taking the phone away for a month: but this leaves little incentive to do better in the future. It makes better sense for a first offence to take the phone away for two days. Make it longer for second and third offences.

THE FAMILY CAR.

Your teen will have unlimited rights to a car only when he buys and maintains his own. Use of the car is a privilege based on the responsibility he demonstrates in other areas of his life. Before a teenager begins driving, parents should draw up a driving agreement. This driving agreement would cover such issues as when the car is available for use (only after permission is granted and homework and household chores are completed), mobile phone use while driving, listening to the radio or CDs while driving, allowing others to drive the car, how many passengers (if any) are allowed, and responsibility for petrol, care, upkeep and insurance costs.

Following discussion and input from both of you, these issues and any more you wish to add can be combined into an agreement which you both sign before your teen begins driving. The privilege of using the car is a powerful motivator towards good behaviour, and withholding the use of the car is equally effective for bad behaviour.

PARENTING: THE BEST THAT YOU CAN BE

VIDEO GAMES.

It is a parent's duty to monitor all types of entertainment played, watched or listened to in the home. This includes such things as television, movies, DVDs, music, computers and video games. Parents are the gatekeepers of what comes into their home.

Most teens consider playing video games as just another recreational activity. But playing video games is an isolating activity and also addictive. A Simon Fraser University study, 'Video Game Culture', revealed that one out of four teens admitted feeling addicted to them and was troubled over his lack of control in playing games. This same study also showed that, where players assumed identities and interacted with other players online, they became so immersed in the game that homework and other responsibilities were neglected. One such game, **World of Warcraft,** has some ten million devotees who pay a monthly subscription fee and spend more than twenty hours a week playing the game. [10]

The National Institute on Media and the Family reports that teens who play violent video games do worse in school than teens who don't. At-risk teen boys spend 60% more time playing games and prefer violent games. Youths who prefer violent games are more likely to get into arguments with teachers, as well as physical fights, whether they are boys or girls.

Another survey suggests that one in twelve teens shows signs of behavioural addiction. Teens participating in the survey admitted to skimping on chores and homework, lying about how much they play, poor performance on homework tests, and unsuccessful struggling to cut back on video game playing.

If you are concerned about the amount of time your teen is spending playing video games, you need to set limits on how much he can play. Then encourage him to get active in other activities.

COMPUTERS AND THE INTERNET.

Computers with internet access hold special dangers because predators routinely scan chat rooms and instant messaging, email or discussion boards to establish contact. Many teens use online peer support to deal with their problems. One study showed that only about 40% of parents review whom their kids are contacting or what messages are being sent.

Young people have easy access to movies with graphic violence. Most parents don't understand the rating systems, and even when they do teens can easily sneak into cinemas or rent DVDs of their choice. Studies show that the more television and movies watched, the lower the age for the first sexual encounter. Not only do studies show it, children themselves report that the media encourages them to begin sexual activity at an early age.

The majority of teens think of networking online as a fun and innocent pastime. But it's up to parents to monitor. Investigate your teen's profile. Many kids have more than one online profile, so find out how many your teen has and where they are. You are entitled to know. Warn your teen not to post anything publicly that parents, predators or principals shouldn't see. Pictures of being drunk or doing drugs at a party might even affect whether they get into college or get a job.

DATING AND SEXUAL BEHAVIOUR.

Teenagers often think they have the right to date when they hit 15 or 16. No! Dating is a privilege depending on their age and maturity and willingness to accept responsibility for their behaviour. The trend today is for young people to date at earlier and earlier ages. Many say they have already dated by ages 12 or 13. Since the average girl reaches puberty at 12.6 and a boy at 13.5, a considerable number are dating and going steady before they reach puberty.

Most teen girls think themselves ready to date by ages 12 or 13. But smart parents will hold their girls back. The younger a girl begins to date, the more likely she is to have sex before graduating from high school. Early dating really can have a massive impact on a girl's life.

The age at which they begin dating affects the likelihood that they will have sex before graduation.

Obviously, the younger a girl begins to date, the more likely she is to become sexually active. This is also true of boys and girls who go steady in the ninth grade. Girls who first have sex at age 15 or younger are almost twice as likely to become pregnant within the first six months of sexual activity as those who wait till they are 18 or 19. This is related to their ignorance about birth control and their level of maturity.

Parents also need to monitor girls dating older men. A large majority of teen pregnancies are caused by males over the age of 20. When a girl is 12 and pregnant, the father is usually around age 22. When a girl is 13 or 14 and pregnant, the father is usually 18 to 20. [11]

In one of the most powerful reports ever published about issues that affect young adults negatively, four top risk factors for sexual involvement were identified and are the same for boys as for girls – alcohol use, a steady boyfriend or girlfriend, no parental monitoring, having parents who think adolescent sex acceptable.

Maybe you think that your teens won't listen to anything you have to say about dating, love or sex. But this report identifies the influence of parents as key to avoiding risky behaviours.

PARENTING: THE BEST THAT YOU CAN BE

> **This study found that parental attitudes play a protective role in delaying sexual activity.**

Young adults responded positively to parental messages when feelings of warmth, love and caring were present.

> **One important study, conducted by Drs Sharon White and Richard DeBlassie and published in Adolescence, found that parents who set the most moderate and reasonable rules for their teens in dating got the best results, in contrast to those who were overly strict. Unsurprisingly, those who provided no guidelines whatsoever were the least effective. But there is no sex-education programme, no curriculum, no school that can match the power and influence of parental involvement. And teens who have a strong religious conviction and participate actively in church are, as a group, far more likely to practise abstinence than their peers.** [12]

It is normal, natural and healthy for teens to show an interest in the opposite sex during these years. But if early dating isn't the answer, what is? Every church and home should provide regular recreational activities for young adults so they can be with the opposite sex. These gatherings can allow for some pairing off, but there should be no 'dating' during the early teen years. Families can get together at one another's home, plan a trip to the mountains, go on a picnic, go skating together or foster any number of activities that allow mixing under controlled circumstances. Church and school activities can supplement the activities planned by parents.

The emphasis should be on being together in a relaxed and healthy atmosphere that adults can properly supervise. This leaves couple dating where it belongs, with those aged 16 and older.

BIZARRE CLOTHING OR APPEARANCE.

If you try to prevent your teen from looking like all the other teens in his school, you are doomed to failure. He dresses the way he does to look different from you and just like his peers. The more you oppose each new craze, the stronger he'll embrace it.

> **As much as possible allow your teen to wear what is important to him, remembering he is searching for acceptance from his peers.**

Should his clothes get too bizarre, his peers will tell him. They can accomplish what you cannot, and more quickly.

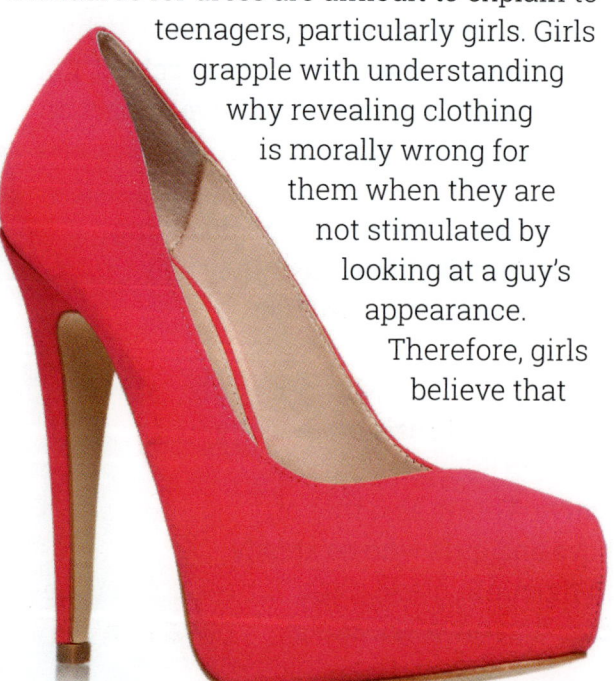

One exception is clothing that is morally wrong — when it is too revealing, too tight, too short, or lacks or shows undergarments. Standards for dress are difficult to explain to teenagers, particularly girls. Girls grapple with understanding why revealing clothing is morally wrong for them when they are not stimulated by looking at a guy's appearance. Therefore, girls believe that guys should not be stimulated by what they see. Girls must be gently taught that they are responsible for the messages they send to guys through their dress: and that guys read sexual come-ons into a girl's appearance.

If it is nothing more than a teen fad, allow your teen to dress like others. But if it is morally wrong, then stand like a rock.

BODY PIERCING AND TATTOOS.

The surging popularity of tattoos can be largely attributed to their taboo status. Piercing of the eyebrows, nose, cheeks, tongue, navel and genitals is on the rise. Piercing is a sign of rebellion, a thrill similar to drag racing or bungee jumping. Should you freak out over a piercing or tattoo, its purpose will truly be fulfilled. Teens love to shock adults and show they have total control over their bodies.

Tongue piercings are dangerous as the teen can accidentally bite on the steel ball and break a tooth. The puncture wound in the tongue is also open to hepatitis and AIDS. A recent study suggests that students with piercings were more likely to have smoked, used alcohol and drugs, had sex, skipped school and become involved in fights. [13]

Young people also do not realise that body piercing and tattoos have pagan roots. It is normal for teenagers to express themselves through what they wear and how they look, but that tattoo will be there long after the fad fades. Discuss with your teens what an employer might think when they apply for a job in a few years.

Through all the difficult years of setting limits on teen behaviour, keep in mind the ultimate goal which your teen is not yet capable of understanding – building inner character. Your teen needs to know that you take no pleasure in restricting his privileges and ruining his day. Keep in mind that the goal of setting good boundaries is to teach self-control, which in turn develops godly character. Your teen may not vote you 'parent of the year', but later in life he will appreciate what you were doing for him.

PARENTING: THE BEST THAT YOU CAN BE

How to motivate an unco-operative teen

The most effective method of getting an unco-operative, lazy, misbehaving or defiant teen to co-operate can be found in withdrawing or manipulating privileges usually granted him. When you've found he's lied about where he was after school, his grades are dropping, or homework or household chores are not being completed when they should be: here's the answer. Nagging, complaining and begging are totally ineffective and will more than likely stir up resistance. But depriving an unco-operative teenager of computer time, the mobile phone, video games or the car now becomes a powerful motivator towards good behaviour. With only a minimum of words, he'll learn he must shape up and that you'll stand your ground until he does.

This is a behaviour modification technique in which the teen earns points for meeting certain obligations during the day and 'cashes in' those points for privileges. There probably isn't a defiant teen alive who will react with great joy over earning points. Explain that it matters to you that the two of you get along better in the future than you have in the past. Mention the chores and obligations that aren't getting tended to. Without getting emotional, state that this may not bother him but it is important to you. Explain that you recognise he obviously needs some motivation to get things done each day and you are prepared to offer that. Mention that everyone is more motivated to get things done when a reward is offered.

Chapter 4 // What counts is character

WHY NOT DO IT THIS WAY?

1. Compile a list of chores or behaviours you want your teen to comply with.
The behaviours listed need to be specific and must be done immediately following your first request. 'Clean your room!' isn't specific enough. Name what part of the room needs to be cleaned. Other requests might include: 'Get up the first time you are called.' 'Make your bed.' 'Start your homework.' List behaviours you want your teen to do – not what you don't want him to do: 'Don't swear.' 'Don't hit your sister.' – and so on, although points can be deducted for negative behaviour. Beware of making this list too easy.

2. Now compile a list of privileges.
What does your teen find highly desirable that he'll want almost on a daily basis? An hour with the TV? Video games? His mobile phone? The family car? Computer time? A ride to an outing or school function? Rank these privileges according to their value to your teen.

If he looks at your list of privileges and says he's always been allowed to watch TV, use the computer, play video games or use his mobile phone, explain that you have allowed him to use these things which you have paid for and maintain: but that you are the one who bought them with your money, and you pay monthly bills to maintain them. Therefore his use of your things is a 'privilege', not a 'right'. Explain that he will get points for complying with requests and obligations which can be used to buy privileges from the privilege list. To head off resistance you can also point out that he can get bonus points if he complies quickly and pleasantly.

PARENTING: THE BEST THAT YOU CAN BE

3. Create a graph of chores/behaviours and privileges on a chart.
Assign point values to each of the requests. A rule of thumb might be 25 points for every fifteen minutes of effort required. You can assign more points for difficult tasks. Now assign privileges on the same scale (25 points for every fifteen minutes of the privilege). Create a new sheet for each day with points earned, points deducted, and a running balance. **Here's a sample:** [14]

Requests Points
Get up on time = 25
Hang up towels after shower = 25
Make bed before leaving bedroom = 25
Brush teeth after breakfast = 25
Put breakfast dishes in dishwasher = 25
15 minutes of after-school studying = 25
15 minutes of listening to classical music = 50
15 minutes of piano practice = 25
30 minutes of work in house or garden without being asked = 100
In bed with lights out at 10.00 = 25
For saying, 'Yes, Mum/Dad, I'd be happy to.' = 50

Day Total Privileges Points
15 minutes on the phone = 25
1 hour of TV time = 100
30 minutes of computer time = 100
30 minutes of video game time = 100
2 hours with the car = 200
Going out for a pizza with the family = 200
Going to the movie with friends = 200
A ride to youth meeting = 50

Chapter 4 // What counts is character

4. Keep a daily running balance.
Every time your teen complies with a request the first time you ask, tell him what he's earned and enter the amount in a 'points earned' column. Award no points if he has to be asked more than once. Make the total points that must be earned reasonable (about two thirds). Note that some of the points that are earned are for weekly privileges: this way your teen can save about one third of his points for that event. Remember to give points if the task is done quickly and pleasantly. You are teaching your teen that positive attitudes and behaviour have positive results.

5. Only you are allowed to enter points on the chart.
Your teen can look at the balance sheet whenever he wants. It could be posted on the refrigerator for easy entering and reference.

6. Stay with it and be realistic.
Point systems, charts and contracts are powerful motivating tools, but only if you stick with them. Beware of backing down from what you've said. Your job at this point is to follow through! Don't start these systems until you are absolutely certain you will follow through. Don't expect too much behaviour change too soon. If you stick with it, your parenting style will become more positive while your teen's behaviour becomes more positive.

WARNING!
It might be that your teen will earn points for a few days, get angry and tear up the chart. You may think the chart isn't working. But it is. Your teen is only testing your resolve to stick with it long-term – a normal reaction for teens. But it can be just as normal for you to enforce the limits you've set.

When nothing seems to work

There are times when nothing we do with our kids seems to work. We try everything we know and don't see any tangible results. Mental and physical exhaustion set in. That's when we want to write the relationship off: 'We did the best we knew how, but it wasn't good enough. So that's the end of it. no more trying to communicate with this defiant kid. It's over.'

This is precisely the time when it's crucial to keep trying. If you keep trying there is still hope of some success. You can always talk to him, whether he wants you to or not. You may have it thrown back in your face. Only later will you be able to see that you did the most important thing, for your teen's sake and for yours. It may be time for you to learn something from your child. Your child may have no intention of letting you be 'normal' parents. If so, there is precious little you can do about it: but good can come from bad. You can learn how to keep the lines of communication open, in spite of everything, because you have to. The only other alternative is to give up on him and your relationship, and that you just can't do.

Footnotes

[1] **Parentwise**, pp. 84, 85.

[2] *www.abelard.org*

[3] Ibid.

[4] Ibid.

[5] Ibid.

[6] Neil Medley, MD, **Depression – the way out**, Ardmore, OK, p. 27.

[7] *http://www.musiceducationmadness.com/important.shtml*

[8] Nedley, p. 210.

[9] Nedley, p. 211.

[10] *www.media-awareness.ca*

[11] Nancy Van Pelt, **Smart Love**, Grantham, Lincolnshire, UK, p. 61.

[12] Nancy Van Pelt, **Smart Love Sexual Values Discussion Plan**, Fresno, CA, p. 2.

[13] *http://www.rense.com/general24/ge.htm*

[14] Russell A. Barkley, PhD, and Arthur L. Robin, PhD, **Your Defiant Teen**, Guilford Press, London, p. 160.

Chapter 5
How to face divorce, single parenting and blended families

> **'The Lord is close to the brokenhearted and saves those who are crushed in spirit.'** Psalm 34:18, NIV

> **'The best time to decide whether you will live the rest of your life together is before you say, "I do", not after!'** Bobb and Cheryl Biehl

You clutch your divorce papers in your hand. At last you are free, free, free! Now you can put the past behind you and look to the future. Or can you?

Many people herald divorce as a remedy for a 'bad' marriage. Yet the joy people expect to experience after their release from a failed relationship doesn't always materialise. Instead, they often experience long-term feelings of bitterness, resentment, and rejection.

One reason divorce is so devastating is because of the rejection that accompanies it. To the same degree that falling in love is exciting, falling out of love can hurt. Divorce is a painful process. Most people agree that divorce is more painful than the death of a loved one. In death the relationship is over and done with. Only memories linger. But in divorce, a relationship still exists – especially when children are shared.

> **Many couples moan, 'If children are involved, divorce is never over!'**

Divorce statistics are rising even among churchgoing families. Christian parents who divorce must answer some serious questions regarding their children. Not only must these children face the dissolution of one home and the creation of a new one with all the necessary adjustments, but these children often have some serious questions about the faith of their parents: 'Why didn't God answer my prayers to keep our family together?' 'Why didn't God help you and Daddy work out your problems?' A child confronted with such a dilemma may become seriously disillusioned with his parents' faith and question whether it is worth it to establish a relationship with a God who seemed unable to help his parents during their time of need. Countless parents have thereby become stumbling blocks to their own children's eternal salvation. And children from divorced

PARENTING: THE BEST THAT YOU CAN BE

families are more likely to divorce later in life. A high price indeed!

Regardless of the problems you face, heed the flag of caution. Look before you leap. Divorce is not always liberating, but, if you are in a situation where divorce cannot be avoided, or if you have been the unwilling victim of circumstances, do not allow these circumstances to defeat or permanently discourage you. Use your past experiences as steppingstones to personal growth. Such an approach will provide a powerful modelling example for your children and others as to how faith works.

Do broken homes produce broken children?

Two weeks before her divorce was to become final, a friend called to update me. 'How are things going?' I queried cautiously.

'Great. Just great. I have peace for the first time in years. Things couldn't be better,' she responded.

Our conversation then drifted to 6-year-old Scott, whose custody she had voluntarily given to the father. She admitted concern. 'He's doing better than he was. He had a lot of stomach pains, so his father and I have been taking him to a psychologist. The sessions have helped. The pain in his tummy and the nightmares are subsiding.'

> **I felt like saying to her, 'What your child needs right now is not a psychologist, but a mother and father and a secure home.'**

Divorce will always have a damaging effect on children, and it is time for adults to stop playing the game of denial. Yes, children are resilient, but this does not mean that they are not seriously affected by the break-up of their homes. Even children who show no outward symptoms during or after a divorce can be affected. The time has come for a realistic appraisal of the effect of divorce on children.

According to Dr H. Norman Wright, psychologist and eminent Christian family counsellor, research illustrates that a child of parents who are going through a divorce experiences the same stages of grief that he would if a parent had died! Furthermore, few children are warned that a divorce is about to take place. About 80% of all children are not prepared in advance of the event.

> **Even when the news is broken gently, the child experiences shock, depression, denial, anger, fear, and a haunting obsession that he might have been responsible.**

Some children cope well and thrive successfully but, as a group, the children of divorce are at serious risk. They are more depressed and aggressive towards parents and teachers, and are more likely to develop mental and emotional disorders later in life. They start sexual activity earlier, have more children out of wedlock, abuse drugs more frequently, are more involved in crime, and

Chapter 5 // How to face divorce, single parenting and blended families

are more likely to commit suicide. They are less likely, when grown, to want to support their parents in old age, which indicates that resentment from the divorce lingers for years. The stigma of divorce may have been removed, but the massive effects remain.

Judith Wallerstein is a psychologist who has been studying the effects of divorce on the same children over the long term. Wallerstein has reached deeper into the psyche of children of divorce over a longer period of time than any other researcher. She says that their parents' divorce hangs like a cloud over their lives – even into adulthood. Her work shows deep and long-term emotional problems, called the 'sleeper effect', that arise only when the children enter early adulthood and begin to confront issues of romance and marriage. Now the 'ghosts' from their parents' experience rise to haunt them. Some of these children, now adults, are more erratic and self-defeating, which is evidenced by them seeking unreliable partners or dull ones (who would at least never leave them). Others ran from conflict or avoided relationships entirely. Expecting disaster, they often worked to create it. Some did experience success in work or romance, but lived with a sense of foreboding that at any moment any happiness or success achieved could vanish. The work of Wallerstein and others undercuts the notion that divorce saves children from the open conflict of parents.[1]

When a divorce is hotly contested, where there are custody battles and children are used as pawns or go-betweens, the effects can be worse. The child's normal capacity to cope is more seriously impaired. Furthermore, when parents claim Jesus Christ as their personal Saviour, the confusion and bewilderment resulting over their inability to solve their problems in spite of the spiritual resources available to them is devastating to the child's belief system.

In most cases, the experts say, it takes three to four years before a child can pull herself together after a divorce. This means that, if a child is 4 when the divorce occurs, she will be 7 or 8 before the effects subside – almost half of her eight years being lived in the awful aftermath of divorce.

Sometimes parents feel they are doing the child a favour by providing a new or more peaceful atmosphere. Only 10% of all children of divorced parents report any feelings of relief. And despite feelings of relief, they still have difficulty adjusting to the divorce. Furthermore, most children, even those from very troubled homes, would go to almost any

PARENTING: THE BEST THAT YOU CAN BE

length to get their divorced parents together again. Many children from broken homes share a common fantasy – a miraculous dream that their parents will reunite. Such a fantasy often lives on for years, even into adulthood.

Should a very troubled family stay together for the sake of the children? Divorce is much more widespread than it needs to be. According to Paul Amato and Alan Booth in **A Generation at Risk**, 70% of American divorces are occurring in 'low-conflict' marriages. Only 30% of divorcing spouses reported more than two serious quarrels in a month, and only 25% said they disagreed often. This means that three quarters of these divorcing couples don't even disagree often!

Furthermore, bad marriage can often improve. Few 'bad' marriages remain that bad. If a couple will stick it out for at least five years, they can turn that bad marriage into a very happy one.

> **It is always preferable to save the existing family whenever possible, rather than opt for divorce.**

This choice – looking for ways to solve a troubled family situation – is preferable for all parties concerned. And the theological implications of divorce for a Christian couple have not been considered yet.

Tips for making divorce less painful for children

Divorce is rarely a pleasant experience: and children become an additional complication through the issues of custody and visitation. Although they are young, innocent and powerless, children become active participants in a tug-of-war during a most vulnerable period of their lives – the developmental years. Here are some tips to make the difficult process of divorce less painful for a vulnerable child.

Inform the child.
Whereas a child should not be exposed to all the ugly details of a divorce, shutting a child off from the process leads to feelings of confusion and isolation. The child will often blame himself for the break-up. Without defaming the other parent, give non-blameful reasons behind the divorce. The worst of the emotional baggage that comes with a divorce must be set aside to free the child from feeling caught in the middle or feeling forced to choose between the parents. The present status of your relationship can be stated in a matter-of-fact manner without anger or hostility towards the other parent. Frequent updates should be given regarding any changes in present conditions or future status. The child should be encouraged to ask questions, which promotes open dialogue between you.

Chapter 5 // How to face divorce, single parenting and blended families

Model dignity and respect.
Parents are the child's primary role models and are the prime influence in self-worth and character development. Should you have a build-up of resentment and anger, seek counselling in an environment where you can safely vent, without your children being present to witness. Your children are watching you. Handle all aspects of the divorce process with dignity and respect – respect for yourself and for your partner, who will continue to be their parent even after the divorce. Handling this difficult situation with dignity and respect teaches a powerful lesson in how to handle the tough times in life.

Repair any cynicism.
Cynicism towards marriage or building a new relationship is a common side effect of divorce. When a parent loses faith in marriage, it becomes easy to pass such feelings on to a young, impressionable child. All those going through a divorce need to take time to process the pain, identify their mistakes, and learn from them. The valuable lessons learned now can help build stronger relationships in the future. Don't project your negative attitudes, anger or resentment on to your children. Discuss with them (within appropriate boundaries) the reason your marriage didn't last. But be positive about your future.

Assign a task.
While not making a child a member of your legal team, try to make him feel a part of the transitions that occur following divorce. Should you be forced to move, or change schools or churches, make the child a 'helper'. Ask for opinions. Have him cut money-saving coupons from magazines or newspapers. Or have him search 'apartments for rent' in the newspaper. A child likes to feel important and involved.

PARENTING: THE BEST THAT YOU CAN BE

> **Pay attention.**
> **Through all the emotional upheaval you experience, keep your eyes open for emotional reactions in your child. Your child is going through tough times also. Don't be so distracted by your own pain that you fail to recognise depression, drug or alcohol abuse, or other drastic changes in behaviour. Constant vigilance and open communication remain your best friends for moving the child towards healing.**

The single parent – can one parent do the work of two?

One of the greatest social phenomena in family life today is the number of children living with only one parent. Furthermore, many children who now have two parents have had only one in the past or will have only one in the future as a result of separation, divorce or death. If the present rate continues, almost one in two of all children will live in a single-parent household before they are 18.

Parenting alone is, frankly, more difficult than parenting with a partner. What were shared responsibilities before must now be maintained alone – supporting the family, maintaining the car, entertaining friends, remodelling, home repairs and housecleaning. Then there are all the tasks related to childcare itself – nurturing; discipline; listening; setting limits and rules; settling quarrels; transporting children to school, music lessons, and meetings; helping with homework; family worship; caring for clothing; plus countless other tasks. If you were to ask a two-parent family if both parents kept busy all day, both would insist that they had full-time jobs whether they worked inside or outside the home. Now, however, one partner must shoulder the entire burden. Under such circumstances, home management takes on new meaning and should receive utmost attention.

Whereas all parents care about their children, single parents have a special reason for cherishing their children – in most cases children are all that remains of their family.

> **Divorced single parents frequently hope that successful parenting can in some way compensate for the marriage failure.**

Chapter 5 // How to face divorce, single parenting and blended families

The widowed often commit themselves to their children to show continued fidelity to their former spouses.

In a way, it is easier for single parents to focus on the child's needs because they don't have to divide time between a spouse and a child. But, in so doing, some parents become overly protective. They may also become overly concerned if their child seems troubled. Single parents usually have cause for concern if there has been an upset in the family because of separation, death or divorce. Indications that the child is not doing well include excessive misbehaviour, insecurity, attention-seeking or aggressive behaviour, or declining grades in school.

The single-parent life

Now that the separation/divorce is over, you need to find a way to create a life that is comfortable for both you and your child. Accept the fact that nothing in your life will ever be the same. That statement may seem huge, unfair and unbearable, but it is true. Your marriage did not work and you have parted. Just because it didn't work does not mean that you cannot create another healthy family environment in which to raise your child. You are simply going to rebuild your life and family in a different way.

Your child, however, will continue to need two parents who care and who can work together as parents. Your child will continue to need to have a relationship with both parents. As soon as possible and as much as possible, bury all bad feelings towards the other parent. In order for your child to grow up feeling loved and secure, you must make room in your child's life for the other parent. Your child needs to continue feeling close to you, but also to feel a closeness with the other parent. Keep your feelings of anger, resentment and tangled emotions separate from this. This is what is best for your child.

You and the other parent broke up because you were unhappy and could not fix things. You no longer have to live with this unhappiness on a daily basis. You will feel some anger from time to time, but it no longer has to be a central part of your life.

If you continue to focus on your anger, even if it is well justified, you will never be able to get past it. If you are always angry, it will affect your parenting of your child.

As difficult as the divorce was for you, it has been one hundred times more difficult for your child. When you appear angry your child interprets that anger as directed towards him or her. Furthermore, it takes a lot of energy to be angry all the time.

The other parent is no longer worth all this anger. In the months ahead you are going to have to learn how to steer through difficult situations. You have experienced a lot of grief and pain that you probably didn't deserve. Take time to grieve for what you have lost by attending a divorce recovery class. Then resolve to make a fresh beginning.

PARENTING: THE BEST THAT YOU CAN BE

A new partner

If you have a new partner in your life, do some serious evaluation before involving that person in your child's life. Keep casual dating partners away from your child. Your child has already suffered one serious loss in his life. Don't subject him to a series of losses by becoming attached to someone and then having that person drop out of his life.

If you have a serious relationship with one person, you can introduce this person to your child. But keep displays of affection private until you are very serious.

> **Avoid trying to make your new partner a part of your family too quickly.**

Should a child ask if you are going to get married again, be honest, but avoid details about the relationship. Expect your child to have some mixed emotions about your dating relationships. Since you are responsible for the character and moral development of your child, never should this partner spend the night. Your children either are teenagers or soon will be, and this is hardly a behaviour you want to encourage in their lives. Should you, remembering Matthew 19:3-9, decide to remarry, don't expect your child to be thrilled about it.

Should the child's other parent be dating, stay out of it. You may be feeling hurt and betrayed, but this is no longer your business. Should your child be witnessing inappropriate sexual activity, express your concerns to the other parent. However, don't believe everything your child tells as the gospel truth. Should the other parent remarry, you can expect your child to experience everything from excitement to despair. While your child adjusts to a new step-parent you need to be patient with your child. Remember, no step-parent can take your place.

Many families have so many problems with visitation that they are constantly going back to court. Courts aren't good for anyone and should be avoided. Making sure your child has a decent relationship with the other parent may not be what you really want, but hopefully you recognise by now that it is what your child needs.

> **Visitation isn't about what you need or even what the other parent needs. It's about meeting the needs of your child.**

Your situation will get easier as you live and work with it. Children are resilient and you will see that your child can adjust to the new circumstances and grow with them and through them.

Chapter 5 // How to face divorce, single parenting and blended families

Working mums

Here we'll discuss not the appropriateness of Mum working full-time, but the best way a family can cope when Mum does have regular full-time employment. Single mums who have no other means of support have no choice. Working will be a part of their lives.

What really separates a working mum from the rest of the world? T-I-M-E. The working mum has less time to accomplish the things she must do. Only adequate time management allows her to survive the demands upon her.

If you are a working mum, here are some quick survival tips:

- Set your priorities and simplify your work as much as possible.
- Enlist help from the kids – they can provide more help than you might expect.
- Keep a daily 'to do' list in your day planner and cross off jobs as you complete them.
- Plan rest and recreation away from the home and kids – without feeling guilty. You'll actually become more productive.
- Reward yourself – make it a habit.
- Set aside one night a week as 'fun night' – no heavy work schedule, serve fun foods on paper plates and after the meal play a game together.
- Save some time weekly for important projects or people.
- Remember, it's impossible to complete everything alone.

PARENTING: THE BEST THAT YOU CAN BE

Many busy mums rely on weekly schedules with blocks of time for family activities, routine chores, errands, and leisure activities. It is wise not to schedule the days too tightly. Leave one hour a day of unscheduled time for spontaneity so that efficiency will not defeat its purpose. Buffer time is necessary. Proper scheduling requires trial and error along with practice, but sooner or later you will work the kinks from the system.

Mothers who work by choice often experience more guilt than those who work due to necessity. Children are quick to sense the conflict between a mother's need to fulfil professional ambitions and, at the same time, satisfy child-rearing responsibilities. Two contradictory needs tug at such a mother. She finds herself torn between staying at home and working full-time. Guilt is counterproductive and causes anxiety, depression and chronic fatigue. It will greatly impede the working mother's ability to parent.

Moreover, children quickly learn how to manipulate parents who harbour guilt. A mother's reaction to leaving her child will greatly influence the child's reaction. If Mother feels apprehensive, fearful and guilt-ridden, she will convey these emotions to her child. If a mum decides to join the workforce, from the onset she should cultivate positive feelings about her decision, regardless of the child's age. Working mothers who have arranged for adequate childcare tend to experience the least guilt.

Blended families on a collision course

Blending families sounds like a great idea until you try it. It sounds like a great idea when you have a mum who needs a dad for her kids and a dad who needs a mum for his kids. But when you get to the nitty-gritty of building one family out of two, it gets complicated. Getting married will not solve all your single-parent problems. Instead, you are opening a new can of concerns. When only one partner has children the issues are less complicated, but problems still arise.

It usually takes three to seven years for families to blend. This means your 6-year-old will be a teenager when you finally begin to feel like a family unit. Then you face new issues during the teen years. The following guidelines may bring some relief:

DISCIPLINE YOUR OWN CHILD AT FIRST:

Early on you will have little or no relationship with your spouse's child. This makes it difficult for you to begin telling a child who barely knows you what to do. And if you do you'll meet with strong feelings of resentment. For the first two to three years each parent should discipline his/her own child. Eventually (three to seven years) the family will gel enough so this will not be necessary.

At first this may create problems if one parent is harsher than the other. Parents in blended families need to work together in applying consistent discipline. Imbalance is better, however, than the resentment generated by inappropriate discipline from a step-parent.

Chapter 5 // How to face divorce, single parenting and blended families

MOVE TO A NEW HOME:

The soundest but perhaps most difficult choice to make is starting afresh in a new home. If you move into his home, you'll find that his kids resent having to share their bedrooms, bathrooms and space with the new 'invaders'. Then the 'guest' family never really feels at home. It is much wiser to move into a new home or apartment where you will start your new family together. Together you will make decisions about who belongs where and who gets what space.

DRAW UP A RULEBOOK:

You and your family grew up with many unwritten rules for behaviour – things like what's right and what's wrong, what's courteous and what isn't, what the mum does and what the dad does. But your spouse has lived in a different home with different rules. Talk about what behaviour is acceptable and what is not. And then talk about it some more with everyone present. Get everyone's input into the rights and wrongs of family life. Then actually draw up a set of expectations and responsibilities.

Remember, you do not yet really know what makes your stepchild tick. You may think he's being cheeky when he was only teasing. You may disapprove of something he's always been allowed to do. Talking about it in advance will help.

PARENTING: THE BEST THAT YOU CAN BE

FORGET LOVE AND SETTLE FOR RESPECT:

Your stepchildren may have many reasons to dislike you. They may consider you an intruder who took their other parent away. They may even blame you for causing the divorce. They may have thought you would be like someone else they heard about and you don't meet their expectations. They may dream up dozens of reasons for disliking you. You may love them and try to prove yourself to them, but you probably won't change much if they are nursing a lot of hurt. The more you try to force them to love you, the less they will.

What you should strive for is respect. Don't try to make the step-parent role more than it is. In time love may come, but it can't be forced. In the meantime, you must have some authority over them. Yes, their parent will handle discipline. But, because you are a co-manager of the home, they need to show you respect. You and your spouse should agree on a standard of respect that should be shown.

The best way to win respect is to give it. You may not love your spouse's children as you love your own. You don't have to. Just respect them the way you expect them to respect you. The more you listen to them and treat them respectfully, the sooner they will return that respect. Common courtesy goes a long way.

ALLOW THEM TO GRIEVE THEIR LOST FAMILY:

Either death or divorce ripped their former family apart, then you stepped in and many things have changed. They may have a lot of hurt and anger over the loss of their father or mother. They hoped that a new family might be like the old one but it isn't working out that way. They compare the new family to the old and nothing makes sense. They sometimes fight to hold on to the old memory, especially if they think you are trying to take that memory away.

Grief is normal when people suffer loss. The classic stages of grief are denial, anger, depression and finally acceptance. Allow your kids time to go through these stages, remembering that there may be a lot of bouncing around during the journey. They may scream at you for no reason, do all they can to wreck your new marriage hoping your spouse will go back to his former partner, or refuse to participate in family activities.

Through it all remember that you are the mature one. You may grieve over the past too, but maturity will not chain you to the past. You are ready for a new adventure, tough as it may be at times.

Footnote

[1] Judith S. Wallterstein, **The Unexpected Legacy of Divorce: The 25-year Landmark Study**.

CHAPTER 6

A good plan for smart families

> 'He will turn the hearts of parents to their children and the hearts of children to their parents...' Malachi 4:6, NRSV

> 'The family is one of nature's masterpieces.' George Santayana

A man came home from work late again, tired and irritated. He found his 5-year-old son waiting for him at the door.

'Daddy, may I ask you a question?'

'Sure, what is it?' replied the man.

'Daddy, how much money do you make an hour?'

'That's none of your business! What makes you ask such a thing?' the man said angrily.

'I just want to know. Please tell me, how much do you make an hour?' pleaded the little boy.

'If you must know, I make $20 an hour.'

'Oh,' the little boy sighed, head bowed. Looking up, he asked, 'Daddy, may I borrow $10 please?'

The father was furious. 'If the only reason you want to know how much money I make is just so you can borrow to buy a silly toy, then march yourself off to your room and get to bed. Think about why you're being so selfish. I work long, hard hours and don't have time for childish games tonight.'

The little boy quietly went to his room and shut the door.

The man sat down and started to get even madder about his son's questions. How dare he ask such questions only to get some money? After an hour or so, the man had calmed down and started to think that he may have been a little hard on his son. Perhaps there was something the boy really needed to buy with that $10, and he really didn't ask for money often.

'Are you asleep, son?' the father asked from the door to his son's room.

'No, Daddy, I'm awake,' replied the boy.

'I've been thinking, maybe I was too hard on you earlier,' said the man. 'It's been a long day, and I took my aggravation out on you. Here's that $10 you asked for.'

The little boy sat up, beaming. 'Oh, thank you, Daddy!' he exclaimed. Then, reaching under his pillow, he pulled out more crumpled-up bills. The man, seeing that the boy already had money, started to get angry again. The little boy slowly counted out his

101

PARENTING: THE BEST THAT YOU CAN BE

money, then looked up at his dad.

'Why did you want more money if you already had some?' the father demanded.

'Because I didn't have enough, but now I do,' the little boy replied. 'Daddy, I have $20 now. Can I buy an hour of your time?'

Time with Dad

Whereas girls, too, need time with their fathers, boys are especially in need of time with Dad. James Dobson in **Bringing Up Boys** says: 'Boys, when compared to girls, are six times more likely to have learning disabilities, three times more likely to be registered drug addicts, and four times more likely to be diagnosed as emotionally disturbed. They are at greater risk of schizophrenia, autism, sexual addiction, alcoholism, bed-wetting and all forms of antisocial and criminal behaviour. They are twelve times more likely to murder someone, and their rate of death in car accidents is greater by 50%. Seventy-seven percent of delinquency-related court cases involve males.

'There is more. Boys younger than fifteen years of age are twice as likely to be admitted to psychiatric hospitals and five times more likely than girls to kill themselves. Fully 80% of suicides involve males under 25 years of age. Suicide among black adolescent boys has increased 165% just in the past twelve years. Boys comprise 90% of those in drug treatment programmes and 95% of kids involved in juvenile court.' [1]

It has also been noted that from lower school through high school boys have lower grades than girls. Boys also account for two thirds of the students in special education classes. Boys are now pursuing fewer graduate degrees than women. Boys have more difficulty in adjusting to school, are ten times more likely to suffer from hyperactivity than girls, and account for 71% of all school suspensions. [2]

Dr William Pollock, Harvard psychologist and author of **Real Boys**, concludes that divorce is difficult for

Chapter 6 // A good plan for smart families

children of both sexes but it is devastating for males. He says the basic problem is the lack of discipline and supervision in the father's absence and his unavailability to teach what it means to be a man. Because boys spend up to 80% of their time with women, they don't know how to act as men when they grow up. When this happens, the relationship between the sexes is directly affected. Men become helpless and more like big kids. Pollock also believes fathers are crucial in helping boys to manage their emotions. Without the guidance and direction of a father, a boy's frustration often leads to varieties of violence and other antisocial behaviour. [3]

Numerous researchers agree that losing a dad (or never having one) is catastrophic for males.

Thirty years ago it was believed that poverty and discrimination were primarily responsible for juvenile crime and other behavioural problems. We know now that divorce is more often the real culprit.

There are two critical periods during childhood when boys are particularly vulnerable. The second is during the onset of puberty. A divorce at that time, more than at others, is typically devastating to boys. The first is between the ages of 3 and 5, when boys gradually pull away from Mummy and sisters in an effort to formulate a masculine identity. During those years, boys crave the attention and involvement of their dad and try to emulate his behaviour and mannerisms. [4]

When dads are absent, inaccessible, distant or abusive during these critical years, their boys have only a vague notion of what it means to be male. Girls have a ready role model in their mothers. The high incidence of homosexuality occurring in Western nations could possibly be related, at least in part, to the absence of positive male influence when boys are moving through these early years. Boys need a clear understanding of their gender assignment and to understand what it means to be a man. [5]

In South Africa, the Pilanesberg National Park rangers have reported that young bull elephants have become increasingly violent in recent years – especially to white rhinos. Without provocation, an elephant will knock a rhinoceros over and then kneel and gore it to death. This is not typical elephant behaviour and was difficult for rangers to explain.

PARENTING: THE BEST THAT YOU CAN BE

The game wardens think they have solved the mystery. Such aggressiveness is a by-product of government programmes designed to reduce elephant populations by killing the older animals. Almost all of the young 'rogue elephants' were orphaned when they were calves, depriving them of adult contact. Under normal circumstances, dominant older males keep the young bulls in line and serve as role models for them. In the absence of that influence the young bulls grow up to terrorise the rhinos. The absence of early supervision and discipline can be catastrophic for boys as well as elephants!

What accounts for the rising number of males who simply can't make it in today's world? Boys are experiencing a crisis in their self-worth that reaches deep within. Many of them are growing up in fatherless homes and finding themselves drifting aimlessly while nurturing the belief that they are not loved by their parents and often ignored or disliked by their peers.

> **This lack of self-worth often acts as a precursor to drug abuse, promiscuity, suicide and violence.**

Prisons hold mostly men who were abandoned or rejected by their fathers.

The author of **Twenty-One Stayed** tells the story of twenty-one American soldiers who were captured by the communists during the Korean War and who later defected to their captors. They chose not to return to the US after the truce was signed. Research by the author revealed that nineteen of the twenty-one soldiers had felt unloved or unwanted by their fathers. A child is not likely to find a Father in God unless he first finds something of God in his father.

Girls and fathering

'What about girls and their fathers?' you ask. Girls who have close positive relationships with their parents during the first five years of life experienced later puberty compared to girls who had more distant relationships with their parents. Girls who entered puberty later had fathers who were active participants in care-giving, and had positive relationships with their mothers. Girls raised in homes where the fathers were absent also entered puberty earlier. The absence of fathers early in a girl's life is a significantly high risk factor for early sexual activity and adolescent pregnancy. Girls whose fathers left before the age of 6 had the highest rates. [6]

Girls in grades eight through to twelve who were not close to their fathers demonstrated a depressed mood in other studies.[7] Fathers also teach their daughters how they can expect to be treated by males when they get older. Fathers teach girls by the way they speak and act towards them and through their treatment of other females, particularly their own wives.

Adolescent girls without fathers in the home behave differently around boys when they have not learned how to act and dress from their fathers. In other words, girls learn how to interact with boys by interacting with their fathers. When a girl overdoes it with provocative behaviour – in the way she walks, talks or dresses – she may be showing that she is starved for the male attention she never got at home due to an absent father – usually caused by divorce or separation.

Girls from homes where parents are divorced are often aggressive with the opposite sex. Their behaviour is seductive and often promiscuous. This results from the tension such young women feel with the opposite sex, tension they act out. They find it difficult to relate easily and openly with boys, and respond more flirtatiously.

Johns Hopkins University researchers found that 'young white teenage girls living in fatherless families . . . were 60% more likely to have had intercourse than those living in a two-parent home'. [8]

Girls without fathers seem desperate to 'connect', and they use sex as the connection. Young women who are emotionally needy but don't know how to engage a man verbally or emotionally often approach him sexually. The danger of such behaviour is more profound than merely shocking the neighbours. Since these young women aren't emotionally ready to handle the psychological ramifications of sex, they learn only how to relate to men sexually. And girls who learn only how to relate to men sexually often make pitifully poor marriage partners and inadequate mothers, who are likely to lead their own daughters into the same type of behaviour.

And girls who don't have effective male role models during their early-to-mid-teen years are highly likely to become vulnerable to the attention of older men, from whom they seek 'fathering' as much as they seek romance and intimacy.

Girls whose parents are separated or divorced are three times as likely to be sexually permissive as girls from intact homes. Girls from such homes reflect the example and teaching of their parents. Girls reared in foster homes, or by guardians other than their parents, are often very sexually aggressive with boys. Strong moral convictions and a desire to live right are developed in a home with affectionate parents, who consistently teach positive values and encourage their teenagers to practise abstinence in their dating relationships. Young people from happy homes are much less likely to be sexually permissive.

Good fathering does matter. It matters for boys, yes, but also for girls.

In conclusion

It is natural for each one of us to strive to be the 'perfect parent'. But, to be totally realistic, perfection in parenting is an unattainable goal. Improvement, however, is realistic. Strive then for little improvements. Each small improvement is a positive step forward, in the right direction. So when you try a new method, and it works, be happy!

Footnotes

[1] James Dobson, **Bringing Up Boys** (Wheaten, Il: Tyndale house), pp. 33, 34.

[2] Michael Gurian, **The Wonder of Boys** (New York: Penguin Putnam).

[3] Dobson, p. 56.

[4] Idem, p. 58.

[5] Ibid.

[6] *http:www.sciencedaily.com/ releases/1999/09/990927064822.htm*

[7] *http://Findarticles.com/p/articles/ mi_m1272/is_n2572_v121/ai_13358877? – accessed online 2011.*

[8] Ibid.

Index

Acceptance 18, 30, 31, 32, 82
Addiction 24, 25, 37, 102
Adoption 22, 23
Affirmation 30, 68
Anger 24, 25, 29, 44, 47-49, 50, 56, 93, 95
Blended family 89, 98
Body image 27, 28
Body piercing 83
Bonding 22
Boundaries 52, 76-83
Boys' statistics 102
Bullying 28, 29, 31
Character 17, 50, 63-88
Charts 68, 69, 85, 86, 87
Communication 11, 39-46, 88, 94
Consequences 11, 12, 41, 57, 58, 70
    Natural 33, 52, 55, 56, 57, 65, 66, 70, 79
Dating 81
Delinquency 13, 102
Depression 25, 27, 29, 52, 78, 94
Discipline 17, 24, 47-62
Divorce 21, 25, 26, 89-95
Eating disorders 28
Empathetic listening 29-31, 41
Fathers and boys 102, 103, 104
Fathering and girls 104, 105
Feelings of worthlessness 17, 22, 23, 26, 27, 28, 31, 36, 42
Habit-forming 63, 66, 68, 69
Hyperactivity 102
Inferiority 15, 16, 18, 20, 35, 36
Internet 78, 80
I-statements 42, 43, 44-46
Labels 21
Maltz's theory 8, 9
Mobile phones 78, 79
Music 77, 78
Neglect 21
Parental fighting 24
Peer pressure 29, 35
Permissive parents 52

Self-worth 11, 15-38
Pre-birth experiences 22
Promiscuity 26, 104
Reinforcement of behaviour 66, 67, 68-72, 84-87
Rejection 20, 21-31, 89
Remarriage 26
Respect 33-37, 39, 40, 49, 61, 66, 76, 93, 100
Security 24, 25, 50, 51, 52
Self-talk 34, 35
Sexting 79
Sexual behaviour 81, 82
Sibling rivalry 48
Slow learner 35
Sources of parental rejection 21-27
Stimulation 21
Strong-willed child 58, 59
Suicide 29, 77, 78, 91, 102, 104
Tattoos 83
Texting 78, 79
Trust 19, 20, 24, 40, 55
TV influence 73, 74
Unwanted children 22, 23, 104
Video games 73, 74, 75, 76, 80
Working mums 97, 98

Juicing for Life

Beverley Ramages has become a regular fresh juice and smoothie maker, and this publication showcases over a hundred of her favourite recipes.

Along with these healthy, easy-to-make and tasty recipes, there is useful information on:
- Selecting the right equipment to get started,
- The values and benefits of the ingredients, and
- The health benefits of each recipe.

All of which will be useful as you begin to develop drinks for your own requirements – for example:
- Weight loss or gain,
- Energy boosting,
- Detoxing, or
- Ensuring that your family get their five-a-day.

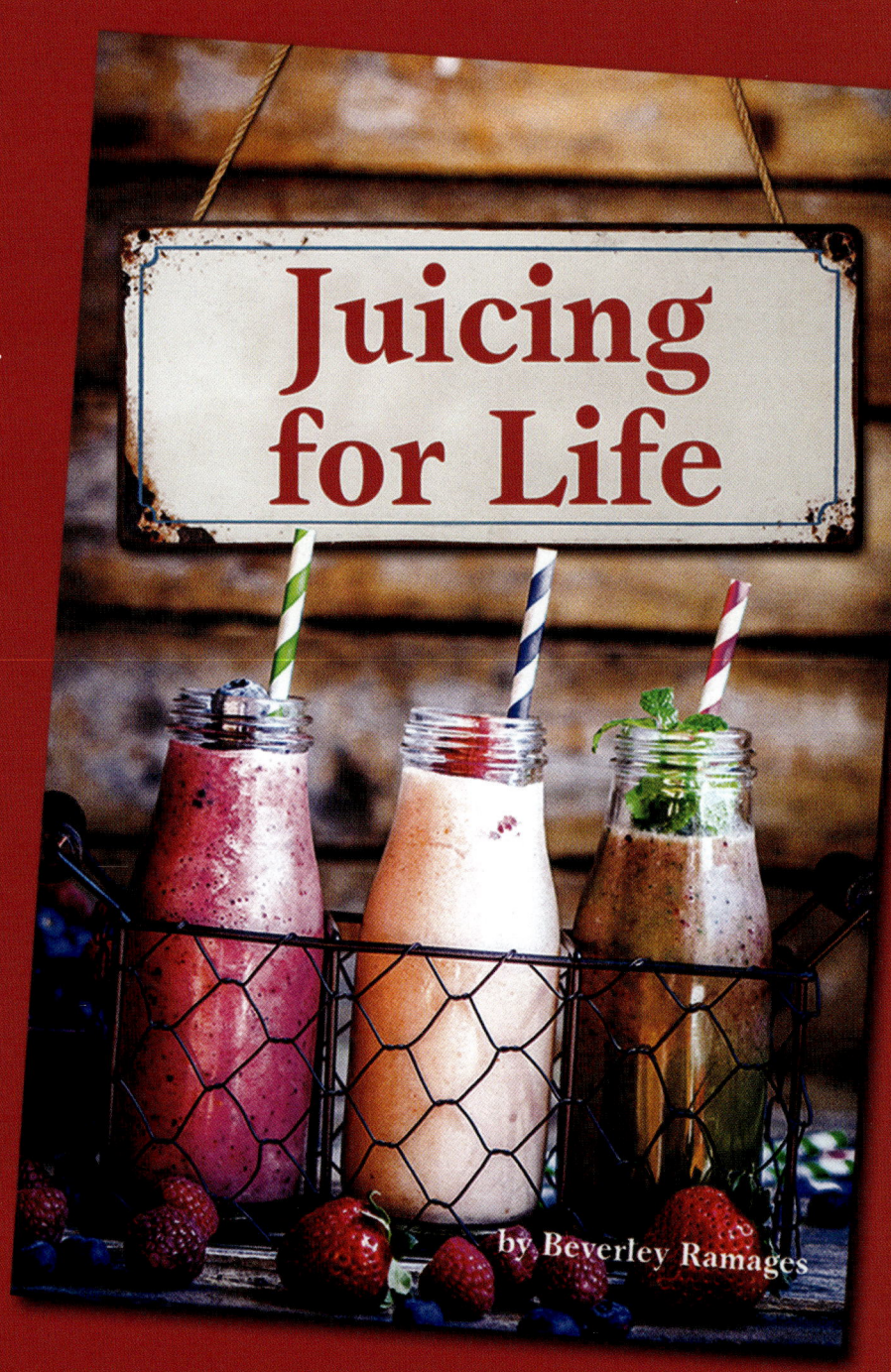

The Stanborough Press Ltd

Your Health In Your Hands

Lifestyle diseases are the biggest killers the Western world faces – and they're of increasing concern for the developing world, too. Your health, and the health of your family, is increasingly a matter of choice, not chance. Find out more about how to choose wisely in this fascinating book originated by a team of doctors and healthcare professionals.

The Stanborough Press Ltd

Eating for Life

Eating for Life

Clemency Mitchell

Additional contributors: Lucinda Annan, Agnes David, Angeline Francis, Huldah Ogwel, and Thelma Soremekun

Eating healthily needn't be boring – or expensive! This book brings practical vegan cooking and baking to life. It is jam-packed with mouth-watering recipes and food-preparation tips for every occasion, from breakfast to supper and from starters to desserts.

You couldn't wish for a more helpful book when it comes to healthy food preparation. Most of the ingredients are readily available, and every one of these recipes is free of animal products – no meat or dairy produce here! What's more, the author places great emphasis on using whole foods, making this book less about what good cooking doesn't contain, and more about what it does – namely, wholesome, nutritious, tasty goodness, just the way it was intended to be.

The Stanborough Press Ltd

Understanding Nutrition

Dr Clemency Mitchell has had 30 years in general medical practice, even longer teaching college students health principles, running health, nutrition and cookery courses.

'My years in general practice taught me that a change in diet and lifestyle would be by far the best prescription for most chronic health problems,' writes Dr Mitchell.

'Nowadays we are bombarded with information about health, including numerous nutritional theories that often seem to change from day to day.'

She continues, 'The principles underlying this book are not based on such shifting sand but on the age-old principles of the Bible, in particular the story of Creation in the book of Genesis where we learn that the Creator designed a plant-food diet and an active lifestyle with a weekly rest day for the human race.'

She concludes, 'Medical and nutritional science, common sense and experience both in the kitchen and the consulting room confirm that these principles still hold the secrets of good health.'

The Stanborough Press Ltd